The Final Atonement of Christ

by

Mark Shipowick

TEACH Services, Inc.
PUBLISHING
www.TEACHServices.com • (800) 367-1844

World rights reserved. This book or any portion thereof may not be copied or reproduced in any form or manner whatsoever, except as provided by law, without the written permission of the publisher, except by a reviewer who may quote brief passages in a review.

The author assumes full responsibility for the accuracy of all facts and quotations as cited in this book. The opinions expressed in this book are the author's personal views and interpretations and do not necessarily reflect those of the publisher.

This book is provided with the understanding that the publisher is not engaged in giving spiritual, legal, medical, or other professional advice. If authoritative advice is needed, the reader should seek the counsel of a competent professional.

Copyright © 2024 Mark Shipowick
Copyright © 2024 TEACH Services, Inc.
ISBN-13: 978-1-4796-1708-1 (Paperback)
ISBN-13: 978-1-4796-1709-8 (ePub)
Library of Congress Control Number: 2024903227

All scripture quotations, unless otherwise indicated, are taken from the King James Version.

Scripture quotations marked ESV are taken from the ESV® Bible (The Holy Bible, English Standard Version®). ESV® Text Edition: 2016. Copyright © 2001 by Crossway, a publishing ministry of Good News Publishers. The ESV® text has been reproduced in cooperation with and by permission of Good News Publishers. Unauthorized reproduction of this publication is prohibited. All rights reserved.

Scripture quotations marked LITV are taken from Green's Literal Translation (LITV). Scripture quoted by permission. Copyright 1993 by Jay P. Green Sr. All rights reserved.

Scripture quotations marked NKJV are taken from Scripture taken from the New King James Version®. Copyright © 1982 by Thomas Nelson. Used by permission. All rights reserved.

Photo Credits:
Figure 7—Aaron Archuleta, CC BY-SA 3.0 ‹https://creativecommons.org/licenses/by-sa/3.0›, via Wikimedia Commons
Figure 8— Livioandronico2013, CC BY-SA 4.0 ‹https://creativecommons.org/licenses/by-sa/4.0›, via Wikimedia Commons
Figure 9— CC BY-SA 3.0, https://commons.wikimedia.org/w/index.php?curid=180955

All other pictures public domain or used with permission.

For more biblical study, see the author's companion book, *Ezekiel's Temple*, **also published by TEACH Services.**

Table of Contents

Introduction		9
Chapter 1	The Ottoman Empire, the Russian Empire, and Gog	12
Chapter 2	The Imminent Coronation of Christ	22
Chapter 3	The Seven Churches Ignited	26
	Joshua and the Angel	28
Chapter 4	Unrolling the Scroll	30
Chapter 5	Revelation's Cleansing of the Sanctuary	33
	The Day of Atonement	36
	Cleansing the Golden Altar	38
Chapter 6	The Unfulfilled Spring Feasts	41
	The Week of Atonement	43
	The Dedication of the Levitical Tabernacle	45
	The Tenth Day of the First Month	46
Chapter 7	The Seven Thunders	48
Chapter 8	The Sixth Seal and the Signs of the End	53
Chapter 9	The Great San Francisco Earthquake	56
	The Great City	58
	Spiritual Babylon	59
Chapter 10	Revelation's Earthquakes	61
	The Shaking Brings Atonement	65

Chapter 11	New York City and 9/11	66
Chapter 12	The Removal of the Testimonies	72
	Silencing the Two Witnesses	79
Chapter 13	Nashville and Great Balls of Fire	80
Chapter 14	Mystery Babylon Rides Again	85
	The Coming Woke Theocracy	85
Chapter 15	Cooperating with Christ	88
	Reaching the Rich	89
Chapter 16	The Abomination of Desolation	91
	The Judgment of Babylon the Great	93
Chapter 17	Who and What Is Babylon?	95
	What's Next?	96
	Seven Mountains	97
	Seven Kings	98
Chapter 18	The Eighth Head and Ten Horns	100
Chapter 19	The 666 Mystery	102
	White and Miller on 666	102
Chapter 20	Lessons from the Rise of Hitler	105
Chapter 21	The King of the North	108
	The Beast and the King of the North	110
Chapter 22	The Strange God of Forces	113
	Armageddon	115
Chapter 23	The Seventh Plague	119
	Propaganda versus Truth	121
Chapter 24	When Michael Stands Up	122
	Numbering Israel Anciently and Today	124

Chapter 25	Loma Linda and the Oath of Michael	127
	The Lord's Oath to Abraham	130
	The Day Before the Great San Francisco Earthquake	133
Chapter 26	When Should We Pray for the Latter Rain?	138
Chapter 27	The Final Victory	143
	The Cleansing of the 2,300 Days	145

Appendices

Appendix A	The Sanctuary Doctrine by J. N. Andrews	147
Appendix B	Time-Setting Statements by Ellen White	151
Appendix C	The Dark Day and Falling of the Stars	154
Appendix D	Thutmose III and the Lateran Connection	158
	The Obelisk of Thutmose III and the Throne	162
Appendix E	153 and 666	164
Bibliography		167
Endnotes		169

Introduction

Behold, the Lord cometh with ten thousands of his saints, to execute judgment upon all, and to convince all that are ungodly among them of all their ungodly deeds which they have ungodly committed, and of all their hard speeches which ungodly sinners have spoken against him.

Jude 14, 15

Repent ye therefore, and be converted, that your sins may be blotted out, when the times of refreshing shall come from the presence of the Lord; And he shall send Jesus Christ.

Acts 3:19, 20

Throughout sacred history, men and women of faith have stood for God under a great variety of challenging circumstances, but today, just before the return of Christ, God's people will be tested by a particular issue: the infamous mark of the beast (see Rev. 13). The mark will be a test to every living soul. It will reveal to mortals and angels who are the goats and who are the sheep—who by faith have accepted the grace of God and been restored to His kingdom by the blood of Christ.

Apart from the Sabbath, the one doctrine that sets Seventh-day Adventists apart from other denominations is the doctrine of the end-time work of Christ for us within the heavenly sanctuary—the investigative judgment. The phrase "investigative judgment" was coined by Adventists to describe Christ's atoning work before His second coming, typified, in the Levitical model, by the Day of Atonement.

Among Adventists, this doctrine creates some trepidation because it includes the idea of coming under the close scrutiny of God Himself. Unfortunately, the process is viewed by many as something like a boy caught with his hand in the cookie jar—or like the giving of the law to Israel when even Moses said, "I exceedingly fear and quake" (Heb. 12:21). However, the purpose of the investigation is atonement. Sin is exposed in the light of the gospel, and the message of the gospel is deliverance and jubilee. The gospel proclaims pardon and liberation for the chief of sinners.

Judgment combined with atonement is, in fact, an ancient scriptural concept, older than the Day of Atonement itself, and one that all the righteous have accepted by faith, from the fall of Adam until today.

"For the time is come that judgment must begin at the house of God: and if it first begin at us, what shall the end be of them that obey not the gospel of God?" (1 Peter 4:17). That is actually good news. Judgment and atonement starts with the household of faith and is the gospel itself.

Why, then, this book? The main purposes and goals of the book are:

1. To provide evidence that we are at the end, and just ahead of us, an overwhelming surprise awaits Western Christianity and the world: judgment day. Just as past civilizations were called to account by God, before Christ returns, He will settle accounts with our generation, placing before men and women the choice between truth and falsehood—the eternal gospel and the mark. This day of reckoning coincides with the final atonement of Christ. God will announce these things by the fulfillment of certain prophecies that need to be understood.
2. To show that God's people are already in the final atonement now, as well as bring attention to the imminent glorification and coronation of the Son that is just ahead. When God honors His Son, the judgment widens to encompass the rest of the secular world.
3. To confirm that many of the prophecies that have been fulfilled in the past are being repeated now in front of our eyes and many more are about to be, and many of these are the most important ones, written especially for us who live in the end times.
4. To stimulate study and discussion of these things and offer suggestions on a methodology for sound, personal study.

> **"**
> *Just as past civilizations were called to account by God, before Christ returns, He will settle accounts with our generation, placing before men and women the choice between truth and falsehood—the eternal gospel and the mark. This day of reckoning coincides with the final atonement of Christ. God will announce these things by the fulfillment of certain prophecies that need to be understood.*
> **"**

While no individual has all the answers, the church collectively will understand all the essential end-time truths before the return of Christ and, by His mediation, be sanctified in and by them.

For non-Adventist readers, one unique feature of the book is its references to the dreams and visions of Ellen White, who lived in the nineteenth and early twentieth centuries and is regarded by Adventists as having the gift of prophecy. These references are not to persuade others of her inspiration; they are given to shed light on the prophecies themselves and encourage their study. The modern prophetic gift is never a substitute for Scripture, but if it is genuine, it is always complimentary—a lesser light pointing to the greater light of the Word.

White stated that we will know where we stand in relation to the end-time prophesies simply by their fulfillment. She assured us that as we see them fulfilled, they will inspire faith in God and interpret themselves. Addressing the church, she encourages and warns us:

> Those who become confused in their understanding of the word, who fail to see the meaning of antichrist, will surely place themselves on the side of antichrist. There is no time now for us to assimilate with the world. Daniel is standing in his lot and in his place. The prophecies of Daniel and of John are to be understood. They interpret each other. They give to the world truths which every one should understand. *These prophecies are to be witness[es] in the world. By their fulfillment in these last days, they will explain themselves.* (White, *The Kress Collection*, p. 105, emphasis added)

The challenge to us today is to identify their fulfillment accurately when they occur. That requires humility and repentance. The careless, proud, and wicked will not understand them (see Dan. 12:10). It also requires a thorough knowledge of the prophecies themselves.

Chapter 1

The Ottoman Empire, the Russian Empire, and Gog

The Ottoman Empire was a vast, prosperous Islamic caliphate that spanned three continents, controlling much of Southeastern Europe, Western Asia, and Northern Africa between the fourteenth and early twentieth centuries. The Ottomans consolidated their power by the overthrow of the Eastern Roman Empire's Byzantium with the conquest of Constantinople, (now Istanbul, Turkey) in 1453. They afterwards dominated the Balkan countries of Southeastern Europe for three centuries and, during this time, were the main barrier to Russian navy access to the Mediterranean Sea via the Black Sea.

The Ottomans were at the peak of their power in the early sixteenth century when the Protestant Reformation awakened a new life and vitality in northern Europe. These nations, in league with those that remained Roman Catholic, gradually reversed the incursions of the Ottomans. Through mismanagement, the caliphate went into further decline, becoming known in the West as "the sick man of the east." On August 11, 1840, the Ottomans surrendered their sovereignty to the great powers of Europe, coming under their jurisdiction and protection.

Shortly before the Ottomans relinquished their sovereignty, Josiah Litch, a Millerite preacher of the second great awakening, had predicted this would happen on that very day based on the prophecy of the sixth trumpet (see Rev. 9). Litch's extraordinary prediction arrested the attention of the Christian world. Here was a small, despised group who showed themselves to be sound expositors of prophecy and Scripture. This

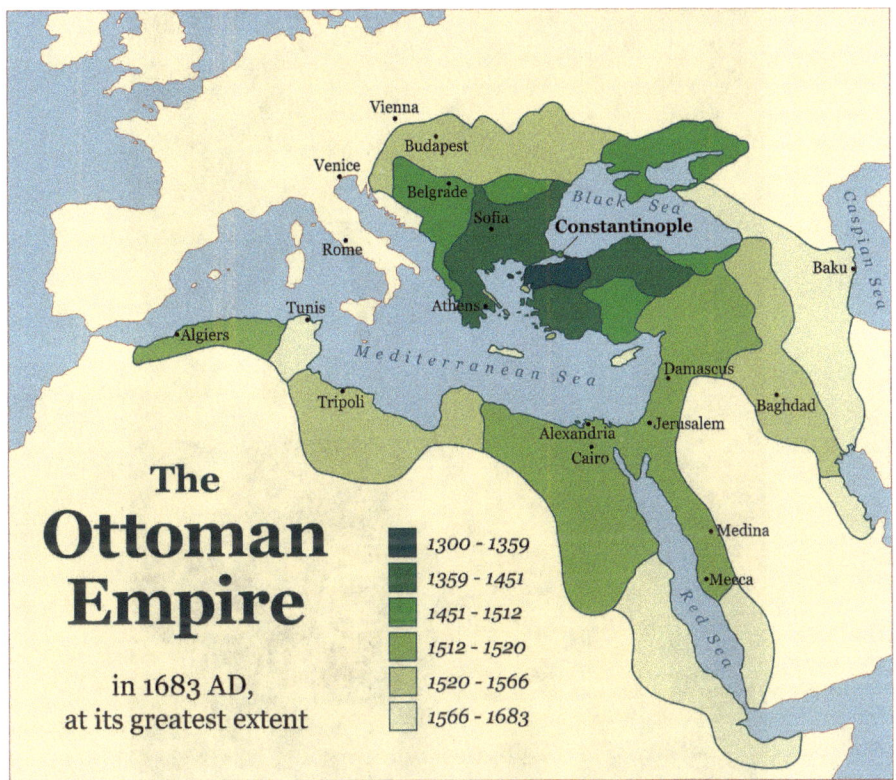

Figure 1: Map of the Ottoman Empire

dramatically increased their credibility and confirmed their faith. Their confidence in God's providential leading in their movement increased, and the revival soon became global.

Fast-forward to today. With the recent war and expansion by Russia into Ukraine, some of the same issues in Europe from past centuries have resurfaced. Turkey, the descendants of the Ottomans, has once again challenged Russian expansion by recently threatening to close the access of the Russian navy again between the Black and Mediterranean seas. The threat to close off access, however, was quite temporary. Since then, although a member of NATO (North Atlantic Treaty Organization), Turkey has realigned itself with Russia and the two have made common cause over Israel's mistreatment of the Palestinians.

At the same time, another grassroots revival had emerged in America, beginning at a university in rural Kentucky in early February 2023,

Figure 2: Siege and Fall of Constantinople, 1453

that, for a time, went viral. Are these and similar developments also a fulfillment of Scripture? Many American Christians see these as signs of the near return of Christ. Let's look at these two briefly—first, Ezekiel's prophecy of Gog and Magog:

> And the word of Jehovah came unto me, saying, Son of man, set thy face toward Gog, of the land of Magog, the prince of Rosh, Meshech, and Tubal, and prophesy against him, and say, Thus saith the Lord Jehovah: Behold, I am against thee, O Gog, prince of Rosh, Meshech, and Tubal: and I will turn thee about, and put hooks into thy jaws, and I will bring thee forth, and all thine army, horses and horsemen, all of them clothed in full armor, a great company with buckler and shield, all of them handling swords: Persia, Cush, and Put with them, all of

them with shield and helmet; Gomer, and all his hordes; the house of Togarmah in the uttermost parts of the north, and all his hordes; even many peoples with thee. Be thou prepared, yea, prepare thyself, thou, and all thy companies that are assembled unto thee, and be thou a guard unto them. (Ezekiel 38:1–7, ASV)

This prophecy is about real nations at the close of human history. It has never been fulfilled; and it says plainly it will happen at the end. Those who have studied ancient history identify the nations listed as follows: Gog, prince of Rosh, is Russia; Persia, Iran; Cush, North Africa; Put, northcentral Africa; Gomer, possibly Poland; Togarmah and Tubal, Turkey. This list appears to be more or less correct in a strictly literal sense. In the prophecy, all these are led by Gog (Russia). If this view is right, it is evident that the invasion of Ukraine is not a good fit so far because none of the above nations except Iran has joined Russia, but that is changing.

The prophecy continues:

After many days thou shalt be visited: in the latter years thou shalt come into the land that is brought back from the sword, that is gathered out of many peoples, upon the mountains of Israel, which have been a continual waste; but it is brought forth out of the peoples, and they shall dwell securely, all of them [Most American Christians see modern Israel as a striking fulfillment of this]. And thou [Gog] shalt ascend, thou shalt come like a storm, thou shalt be like a cloud to cover the land, thou, and all thy hordes, and many peoples with thee. Thus saith the Lord Jehovah: It shall come to pass in that day, that things shall come into thy mind, and thou shalt devise an evil device: and thou shalt say, I will go up to the land of unwalled villages. (Ezekiel 38:8–10, ASV)

The main questions are 1) Is the prince of Rosh literally modern-day Russia or a broader symbol of the forces of evil that unite to attack God's people at the end? and 2) Who are God's people at the end?

> In Scripture, the prophecies that reference world empires are not so much about politics and international conflicts as they are about the role these empires play in the battle between good and evil. There were other empires, such as the Chinese, that existed in ancient times, but these are not mentioned because they had little or no interaction with God's people.

In Scripture, the prophecies that reference world empires are not so much about politics and international conflicts as they are about the role these empires play in the battle between good and evil. There were other empires, such as the Chinese, that existed in ancient times, but these are not mentioned because they had little or no interaction with God's people. Similarly, at the end, the focus is the conflict between spiritual Babylon, the harlot church, the beast she rides that enforces her dogma, and spiritual Israel.

The Scripture definition of the Israel of God is the nation comprised of true Jews who are the children of Abraham by faith. "For he is not a Jew, which is one outwardly; neither is that circumcision, which is outward in the flesh: But he is a Jew, which is one inwardly; and circumcision is that of the heart, in the spirit, and not in the letter; whose praise is not of men, but of God" (Rom. 2:28, 29).

One characteristic of the final coalition of evil is that it originates in the symbolic north. Anciently, Babylon was Israel's northern enemy. This symbol is used in Revelation, but this is clearly spiritual Babylon, the great harlot that fornicates with the kings and nations of the earth,

Figure 3: EU Parliament, Strasbourg, France

not the long-extinct Chaldean kingdom of Nebuchadnezzar. In the end, spiritual Babylon and the beast make war on spiritual Israel, those who "keep the commandments of God and have the testimony of Jesus" (Rev. 12:17). Gog, also a northern power, therefore, is a broader symbol of the combined forces of evil, similar to the adulterous whore.

Historically, resistance to the Ottoman invasion of Europe came from the papacy and the Holy Roman Empire, which eventually included many Protestant nations. Similarly, from the start of the Russian invasion, the pope has been the most active international diplomat. This aligns with the main goal of the papacy: its reestablishment as the head of Christendom over a reunified Europe.

The European Union, like its predecessor, the Holy Roman Empire, has similar aspirations. It's no coincidence that the European Parliament in Strasbourg, completed in 1992, is the only modern structure that is round and intentionally unfinished, mimicking the tower of Babel, the site of antiquity's most glorious empire: golden Babylon.

Note the description of the European Parliament building:

> The 60m high tower, intentionally left unfinished on one side, carries heavy symbolism, and is often said to have been oriented eastwards, i.e. towards eastern Europe, as by the time of the completion of the building no country from the former Soviet bloc had yet joined the EU. However, the open side of the tower actually faces west. In 2010 Glenn Beck suggested that the tower's design consciously mirrors the Vienna painting of the Tower of Babel by Pieter Bruegel the Elder.[1]

The prophecy of the first beast of Revelation 13 is a good fit here, both historically and in what is unfolding now. Originally, the papacy rode the beast, the Roman Empire, for 1,260 years, from the combining of church and state in AD 538 under Emperor Justinian, who granted the pope jurisdiction over the consciences of the people as the corrector of heretics. For the following 1,260 years, the papacy interposed itself between Christ and the people until it was mortally wounded, deposed, and taken captive by Napoleon in 1798.

However, the prophecy says the mortal wound will be healed and the woman will ride again, so in the near future, we can expect the same adulterous relationship between church and state—between the papacy

---

[1] "Seat of the European Parliament in Strasbourg," Wikipedia Foundation, last modified May 2, 2023, https://en.wikipedia.org/wiki/Seat_of_the_European_Parliament_in_Strasbourg

Figure 4: *Tower of Babel* by Pieter Bruegel the Elder

and the leading nations of the European Union (we will come back to this in chapters 17 and 18).

In times of peace, the aspirations of the Vatican and the EU are not front and center in the minds of Europeans, but in the face of Russian aggression and expansion, more Europeans are viewing a reunited Europe under the pope's leadership not so much as a nice ideal but as a matter of survival, especially now that European energy security has been subverted by its main NATO partner, the United States.

In late September 2022, the US sabotaged the Nord Stream pipeline. This story was uncovered by Seymour Hersh, one of the most respected journalists with a long track record of accurately exposing corruption. His account, broadly accepted now, except by Western mainstream media, not only documented in detail how the US did this with the help of Norway but also provided the motive behind it: to ensure Germany remains with them in the conflict with Russia.

The symbolism of the European Parliament building suggests modern Babel will not be complete until all of Europe is reunited. Unfortunately, the Protestant nations of Europe have largely forgotten their own history: It was the Word of God that broke the bonds of superstition and vice and gave vitality to the nations making them models of self-government and self-defense. This denial of the past is rooted in a denial of the Word and has brought Protestantism back to the fold of Rome.

Since the time of Martin Luther, the primary roadblock to European reunification has been Christian fundamentalism—loyalty to God and His Word. The most recent example of this is Brexit. While the Word of God was not the overt cause, its principles were the operative force. Like Britain under Henry VIII, the British spirit, to some extent, still cherishes genuine freedom, which is only found in the gospel.

Whether in Britain, Europe, Israel, or elsewhere, the Word has always acted like salt, preserving the nations, societies, and families wherever it takes root. However, where the Word is denied, courage wanes, nationalism falters, and a socialist, oppressive "common good" takes its place. The gap between rich and poor widens; endemic poverty, enslavement, war, and chaos are the result.

According to the prophecy of Ezekiel, at the end, the hordes of Gog will besiege spiritual Israel—those who "keep the commandments of God, and the faith of Jesus" (Rev. 14:12). If history is an indicator, many British brothers and sisters will take part in this final, global move of God.

Additionally, according to the prophecy of the apostle Paul, the bloodline of Israel will be among the foremost of those who return to God under the latter rain. The prophets and apostles agree that the blindness of literal Israel is temporary. Thank God! The prophecies foretell that many Jews will be enlightened by the gospel of Christ (see Rom. 11:25). One test of the current American revival will be whether it has enough substance to break through Jewish tradition and prejudice. In my view, the revival will need to strike its roots deeper in Christ and Scripture before it can reach our Jewish brothers and sisters.

One means of their enlightenment and ours will be the troubles we will all endure as a result of war and social chaos. As Christ prophesied, there will be global suffering. This will be a means of driving *all* of us to our knees, causing us to call on the Lord. More than a century and a half ago, Ellen White was given a vision of this time:

> I was shown the inhabitants of the earth in the utmost confusion. War, bloodshed, privation, want, famine, and pestilence were abroad in the land. As these things surrounded God's people, they began to press

together, and to cast aside their little difficulties. Self-dignity no longer controlled them; deep humility took its place. Suffering, perplexity, and privation caused reason to resume its throne, and the passionate and unreasonable man became sane, and acted with discretion and wisdom.

My attention was then called from the scene. There seemed to be a little time of peace. Once more the inhabitants of the earth were presented before me; and again everything was in the utmost confusion. Strife, war, and bloodshed, with famine and pestilence, raged everywhere. Other nations were engaged in this war and confusion. War caused famine. Want and bloodshed caused pestilence. And then men's hearts failed them for fear, "and for looking after those things which are coming on the earth." (White, *Testimonies for the Church*, vol. 1, p. 268)

Let's continue with Ezekiel's prophecy:

Sheba, and Dedan, and the merchants of Tarshish, with all the young lions thereof, shall say unto thee [Gog], Art thou come to take the spoil? hast thou assembled thy company to take the prey? to carry away silver and gold, to take away cattle and goods, to take great spoil? Therefore, son of man, prophesy, and say unto Gog, Thus saith the Lord Jehovah: In that day when my people Israel dwelleth securely, shalt thou not know it? And thou shalt come from thy place out of the uttermost parts of the north, thou, and many peoples with thee, all of them riding upon horses, a great company and a mighty army; and thou shalt come up against my people Israel, as a cloud to cover the land: it shall come to pass in the latter days, that I will bring thee against my land, that the nations may know me, when I shall be sanctified in thee, O Gog, before their eyes.... For in my jealousy and in the fire of my wrath have I spoken, *Surely in that day there shall be a great shaking in the land of Israel*; so that the fishes of the sea, and the birds of the heavens, and the beasts of the field, and all creeping things that creep upon the earth, and all the men that are upon the face of the earth, shall shake at my presence, and the mountains shall be thrown down, and the steep places shall fall, and every wall shall fall to the ground [Please make note of this shaking because we'll come back to it in chapters 8 and 9]. And with pestilence and with blood will I enter into judgment with him; and I will rain upon him, and upon his hordes, and upon the many peoples that are with him, an overflowing shower, and great hailstones, fire, and brimstone. And I will magnify myself, and sanctify myself, and I will make myself known in the eyes of many nations; and they shall know that I am Jehovah. (Ezekiel 38:13–16, 19–23, ASV, emphasis added)

Let's stay faithful in these awesome times. We're on the boarders of eternity.

And the Spirit and the bride say, Come. And let him that heareth say, Come. And let him that is athirst come. And whosoever will, let him take the water of life freely.... He which testifieth these things saith, Surely I come quickly. Amen. Even so, come, Lord Jesus. The grace of our Lord Jesus Christ be with you all. Amen. Revelation 22:17, 20, 21

Chapter 2

The Imminent Coronation of Christ

The LORD said unto my Lord, Sit thou at my right hand, until I make thine enemies thy footstool. The LORD shall send the rod of thy strength out of Zion: rule thou in the midst of thine enemies. Thy people shall be willing in the day of thy power, in the beauties of holiness from the womb of the morning: thou hast the dew of thy youth. The LORD hath sworn, and will not repent, Thou art a priest for ever after the order of Melchizedek.

Psalm 110:1–4

And again, when he bringeth in the firstbegotten into the world, he saith ... Thy throne, O God, is for ever and ever: a sceptre of righteousness is the sceptre of thy kingdom.

Hebrews 1:6, 8

Inspiration tells us that humanity, before the return of Christ, will face a "great terror" and an "overwhelming surprise":

> Transgression has almost reached its limit. Confusion fills the world, and a great terror is soon to come upon human beings. The end is very near. We who know the truth should be preparing for what is soon to break upon the world as an overwhelming surprise. (White, *Testimonies for the Church*, vol. 8, p. 28)

The time is nearing when the great crisis in the history of the world will have come, when every movement in the government of God will be watched with intense interest and inexpressible apprehension. In quick succession the judgments of God will follow one another,—fire and flood and earthquakes, with war and bloodshed. Something great and decisive will soon of necessity take place. (White, *Life Sketches of Ellen G. White*, p. 413)

The above paragraphs indicate a future crisis of global proportions will suddenly confront humanity, shaking it to the core. The prophecy indicates this will come in the form of natural and manmade calamities. These conditions are hard for Americans to grasp fully because we have enjoyed unparalleled peace and prosperity for years. However, in the last three years, God, in His mercy, has given us a preview of the calamities that will befall the wicked, unrepentant nations, including America, as Christ makes His final plea for the souls of men and women.

> *In the last three years, God, in His mercy, has given us a preview of the calamities that will befall the wicked, unrepentant nations, including America, as Christ makes His final plea for the souls of men and women.*

We are told in Scripture that fifty days after Christ rose from the grave and ascended to heaven, He was crowned at Pentecost, and the early rain was the result. Similarly, before He returns, He will receive even greater honor when He is crowned the second time, and the latter rain will be given from the royal bounty. Just as David and Solomon were types of Christ and both crowned twice, Christ is also crowned twice in human history.

> Wherefore he saith, When he ascended up on high, he led captivity captive, and gave gifts unto men. (Now that he ascended, what is it but that he also descended first into the lower parts of the earth? He that descended is the same also that ascended up far above all heavens, that he might fill all things.) And he gave some, apostles; and some, prophets; and some, evangelists; and some, pastors and teachers. (Ephesians 4:8–11)

The work of Christ in bestowing the latter rain is symbolized by the ancient Day of Atonement. Like in the Hebrew service that symbolically cleansed the nation, today, Christ is performing a final work of atonement to present His church to Himself "without spot or wrinkle or any such thing" (5:27).

Christ's coronation, mediation, and judgment are also pictured throughout the Scriptures. Daniel 7 and Revelation 4–5 especially reveal what takes place at that time. In both of these parallel descriptions, the heavenly court convenes, and the Son of Man is crowned, glorified, and honored. The coronation scene is impressively pictured as follows:

> I beheld till the thrones were cast down, and the Ancient of days did sit, whose garment was white as snow, and the hair of his head like the pure wool: his throne was like the fiery flame, and his wheels as burning fire. A fiery stream issued and came forth from before him: thousand thousands ministered unto him, and ten thousand times ten thousand stood before him: the judgment was set, and the books were opened.... *I saw in the night visions, and, behold, one like the Son of man came with the clouds of heaven, and came to the Ancient of days, and they brought him near before him. And there was given him dominion, and glory, and a kingdom, that all people, nations, and languages, should serve him: his dominion is an everlasting dominion, which shall not pass away, and his kingdom that which shall not be destroyed....* And at that time shall Michael stand up, the great prince which standeth for the children of thy people: and there shall be a time of trouble, such as never was since there was a nation even to that same time: and at that time thy people shall be delivered, every one that shall be found written in the book. (Daniel 7:9, 10, 13, 14; 12:1, emphasis added)

It would be good to spend some time meditating on these sublime scenes. Here, Christ is given universal authority to bring the plan of salvation to its consummation and establish on earth His eternal kingdom of righteousness. This is a watershed event. Michael, who is Christ, is crowned and stands up in royal authority on behalf of His people[i] (see 12:1). Apart from the cross, there is no greater event in human history. This event is further described in Revelation 6, where, shortly after His coronation, the Lion-Lamb, the King of Judah, opens the seals one by one until the seventh seal, which ends with His advent.

In the following chapters, we will highlight other prophecies that further identify the start of that process of Christ's coronation and atonement, fleshing out the aspects of His intercession that seals the new covenant church so she is adorned in her spotless, dazzling wedding gown.

And I heard as it were the voice of a great multitude, and as the voice of many waters, and as the voice of mighty thunderings, saying, Alleluia: for the Lord God omnipotent reigneth. Let us be glad and rejoice, and give honour to him: for the marriage of the Lamb is come, and his wife hath made herself ready. And to her was granted that she should be arrayed in fine linen, clean and white: for the fine linen is the righteousness of saints.

Revelation 19:6–8

Chapter 3

The Seven Churches Ignited

In Revelation 19, Christ is pictured on a white horse riding into war with the hosts of heaven following Him. This is very similar to the picture of Christ ministering among the seven candlesticks:

> And I turned to see the voice that spake with me. And being turned, I saw seven golden candlesticks; And in the midst of the seven candlesticks one like unto the Son of man, clothed with a garment down to the foot, and girt about the paps with a golden girdle. His head and his hairs were white like wool, as white as snow; and his eyes were as a flame of fire; And his feet like unto fine brass, as if they burned in a furnace; and his voice as the sound of many waters. And he had in his right hand seven stars: and out of his mouth went a sharp twoedged sword: and his countenance was as the sun shineth in his strength. (Revelation 1:12–16)

Notice the similarities between the descriptions: In both passages, Christ is clothed in a dazzling vesture, His eyes are a flame of fire, and a sharp sword proceeds out of His mouth. In Revelation 19, the emphasis is on His kingship as a mighty general and commander of the host. In Revelation 1, the emphasis is on His priesthood.

As we read on, though, the picture of Christ among the lampstands in Revelation 1 changes dramatically in chapters 4 and 5 when He is crowned and asserts His kingly authority:

> And out of the throne proceeded lightnings and thunderings and voices: and there were seven lamps of fire burning before the throne, which are the seven Spirits of God.... And I beheld, and, lo, in the midst of the throne and of the four beasts, and in the midst of the elders, stood a Lamb as it had been slain, having seven horns and seven eyes, which are the seven Spirits of God sent forth into all the earth. (Revelation 4:5; 5:6)

In the passage above, when the Lion-Lamb takes the book, the seven gently burning candlesticks of chapter 1 are replaced by "seven lamps of fire," which are not only intensely brighter but also portrayed as a physical part of Him! The Lamb has "seven eyes which are the seven spirits of God," yet the seven spirits of God are the seven lamps of fire. Combining the two descriptions, inspiration makes the seven lamps of fire, the seven eyes, and the seven spirits of God all equivalent to each other. All are symbols of the same thing: the purified church that operates in full, perfect union with her Lord. She becomes part of Him.

Also notice that in addition to His seven lamps/eyes/spirits, Jesus now also has seven horns. Horns are symbols of power; seven of them is the perfection of power. Here, at His coronation, Christ is invested with all kingly power in heaven and earth—power to unlock the final seven sealed chapters of earth's history and rule until His foes are made His footstool.

> The LORD said unto my Lord, Sit thou at my right hand, until I make thine enemies thy footstool. The LORD shall send the rod of thy strength out of Zion: rule thou in the midst of thine enemies. Thy people shall be willing in the day of thy power, in the beauties of holiness from the womb of the morning: thou hast the dew of thy youth. The LORD hath sworn, and will not repent, Thou art a priest for ever after the order of Melchizedek. The Lord at thy right hand shall strike through kings in the day of his wrath. He shall judge among the heathen, he shall fill the places with the dead bodies; he shall wound the heads over many countries. He shall drink of the brook in the way: therefore shall he lift up the head. (Psalm 110:1–7)

Consider this awesome thought: Christ is crowned a second time at the start of the latter rain by a people who offer themselves willingly. "Thy people shall be willing in the day of thy power, in the beauties of holiness from the womb of the morning: thou hast the dew of thy youth" (verse 3).

In the world, a king is crowned by his willing subjects. In the kingdom of Christ, the same is true, but in a much deeper sense. We offer Him our most complete allegiance, love, and worship. In our enthronement of Him, He, in turn, is enthroned in us—in our hearts and souls. And what a thought it is that we have the honor of participating in His enthronement. This relationship is the most tender, sacred covenant.

This agrees with Zechariah's description of Christ as the royal gemstone with seven facets (or eyes) on which we have been engraved.

> For behold, on the stone that I have set before Joshua, on a single stone with seven eyes [which are the seven lamps of fire and seven spirits of fire (see Rev. 4:5; 5:6)], I will engrave its inscription, declares the LORD of hosts, and I will remove the iniquity of this land in a single day. In that day, declares the LORD of hosts, every one of you will invite his neighbor to come under his vine and under his fig tree. (Zechariah 3:9, 10, ESV)

Notice the seven-faceted stone is engraved by God when the sins of spiritual Israel are removed. And notice they are removed in a single day. What day is that? The antitypical day of atonement—today. This is the fruit of the final ministry of Christ, who silences the accuser of the brethren.

Joshua and the Angel

In the vision above, we have the promise of the complete atonement of Israel. Recall that in this vision, Joshua is the target of Satan's accusations. However, the Lord rebukes the adversary, removes Joshua's filthy garments, clothes him in fair priestly robes, crowns him with a holy crown, and then charges him with his commission, promising him his work will succeed, the sins of Israel will indeed be purged on that day, and she will become a nation of priests where "every one of you will invite his neighbor to come under his vine and under his fig tree."

We find a similar picture in Revelation 3. Here, the name of the seventh and final church, Laodicea, means "a people judged." It parallels Zechariah 3 with the message of Christ to this church: He entreats His people to repent and choose life so their sins are cleansed and they are not judged and spewed out of His mouth.

The message to Laodicea is immediately followed by the judgment scene in the next chapter, where "thrones are set" in heaven and the Ancient of Days presides (see Dan. 7:9); and "out of the throne proceeded lightnings and thunderings and voices" (Rev. 4:5). The result of this atonement and judgment by Christ is the purging of Laodicea: When this occurs, the seven gently burning candlesticks give way to seven blazing torches under the power of the latter rain.

Chapter 4

Unrolling the Scroll

The Scriptures and Ellen White both teach that at the end of time, before the return of Christ, God will break His silence by an overwhelming surprise. When the Lion-Lamb takes the scroll and breaks open its seals, all the world will be arraigned before the bar of infinite justice. Humanity at that point will know beyond a doubt that judgment day has arrived. Unfortunately, most will deny it and not repent.

> The mighty God, even the LORD, hath spoken, and called the earth from the rising of the sun unto the going down thereof. Out of Zion, the perfection of beauty, God hath shined. Our God shall come, and shall not keep silence: a fire shall devour before him, and it shall be very tempestuous round about him. He shall call to the heavens from above, and to the earth, that he may judge his people. Gather my saints together unto me; those that have made a covenant with me by sacrifice. And the heavens shall declare his righteousness: for God is judge himself. Selah. (Psalm 50:1–6)

Speaking of the same event, the unsealing of the scroll, Ellen White made similar prophetic statements:

> When Pilate washed his hands, saying, "I am innocent of the blood of this just person," the priests joined with the ignorant mob in declaring passionately, "His blood be on us, and on our children." Matthew 27:24, 25.

> Thus the Jewish leaders made their choice. Their decision was registered in the book which John saw in the hand of Him that sat upon the

throne, the book which no man could open. *In all its vindictiveness this decision will appear before them in the day when this book is unsealed by the Lion of the tribe of Judah.* (White, *Christ's Object Lessons*, p. 293, emphasis added)

The light that we have upon the third angel's message is the true light. The mark of the beast is exactly what it has been proclaimed to be. *Not all in regard to this matter is yet understood, and will not be understood until the unrolling of the scroll;* but a most solemn work is to be accomplished in our world. (White, *Testimonies for the Church*, vol. 8, p. 159, emphasis added)

At this point, you may be wondering, 'Don't many Christians, including Adventists, teach that the scroll was unsealed centuries ago?' Yes, Protestants taught that for centuries. However, God, through the prophets, would like to expand our view. He tells us this book that is in His right hand contains information about earth's final events, the mark, 666, and the seal of God; He tells us these are important topics we need to understand, but we have more to learn. The question of Sabbath versus Sunday sacredness is a central part of the issue, but there is more to it. The remnant people of God keep not only the Sabbath; they keep all the provisions of the covenant; they are, in fact, sealed in the new covenant by the latter rain and have the testimony of Jesus, which is the spirit of prophecy.

> The question of Sabbath versus Sunday sacredness is a central part of the issue, but there is more to it. The remnant people of God keep not only the Sabbath; they keep all the provisions of the covenant; they are, in fact, sealed in the new covenant by the latter rain and have the testimony of Jesus, which is the spirit of prophecy.

"Judgment begins with the household of God" (1 Peter 4:17), and the Lord, through further inspiration, confirms He is measuring us:

The grand judgment is taking place and has been going on for some time. Now the Lord says, Measure the temple and the worshippers thereof [Revelation 11:1]. Remember when you are walking the streets about your business, God is measuring you; when you are attending your household duties, when you engage in conversation, God is measuring you. Remember that your words and actions are being daguerreotyped [photographed] in the books of heaven, as the face is reproduced by the artist on the polished plate. (White, *The SDA Bible Commentary*, vol. 7, p. 972)

If we put these statements together, they teach that the judgment of spiritual Israel, the church, is an ongoing reality. However, at a certain divinely appointed time, that process expands to include the world, and, like the cross, this transition marks a new era in human history. Just as the events surrounding the crucifixion were plainly foretold by the prophets, especially in Daniel 9, we might expect an event of this magnitude—all the world being arraigned before the bar of God—will be revealed in prophecy with equal clarity.

Ellen White strongly implies that the unrolling of the scroll in Revelation 5 is a description of that event:

The fifth chapter of Revelation needs to be closely studied. It is of great importance to those who shall act a part in the work of God for these last days. There are some who are deceived. They do not realize what is coming on the earth.... *Unless they make a decided change they will be found wanting when God pronounces judgment upon the children of men.* They have transgressed the law and broken the everlasting covenant, and they will receive according to their works. (White, *Testimonies for the Church*, vol. 9, p. 267, emphasis added)

When the Lion-Lamb takes the book and announces its opening seal by seal with a voice of thunder, the judgment turns to the Christian world. Then those who are spiritually awake begin to understand things they haven't understood as God successively removes His hand from the final seven concealed portions of the book. This is when the remaining issues relating to the mark are made plain by the Holy Spirit.

How do we know the Lamb has taken the book? We know by the fulfillment of prophecy: John will "prophesy again" and measure the temple (the church) and those who worship there, and Daniel, like John, will "stand in his lot and place" at the end. Specifically, we will know by 1) the fulfillment of the seals, 2) the voices of the seven thunders, and 3) the sounding of the seven trumpets.[ii]

Chapter 5

Revelation's Cleansing of the Sanctuary[2]

Repent ye therefore, and be converted, that your sins may be blotted out, when the times of refreshing shall come from the presence of the Lord.

Acts 3:19

The Levitical sanctuary service teaches that there are two stages in the purging of our sins: 1) their initial atonement, when we confess our sins and their burden of guilt is removed from us by the blood of Christ; and 2) the final blotting out of their record by Christ from the heavenly sanctuary. The first step is illustrated in the Hebrew tabernacle by the *daily* service. The second is symbolized by the *yearly* Day of Atonement (For a more in-depth explanation, see Appendix A).

Most Christians teach that once a person's sins are confessed, they are removed permanently and thrown into the depths of the sea, never to be remembered again. The Scriptures support that view to a point: When we come to Christ confessing our sins, He blots them from our record with His blood, and we stand free and clear of them before God as though we had never sinned. This is wonderfully good news and central to the gospel.

Nevertheless, the ancient services also teach that when the records of our sins are cleared, they are transferred to heaven's books, where they stay until their final blotting out on the great antitypical day of atonement. At Pentecost, the apostle Peter, full of the Holy Spirit, exhorted his listeners, "Repent ye therefore, and be converted, *that your sins may be blotted out,*

---

[2] This chapter, because of its importance, has also been published in the author's companion book, *Ezekiel's Temple*. It has been edited and enhanced here.

when the times of refreshing [the latter rain] *shall come from the presence of the Lord*" (Acts 3:19, emphasis added).

Notice the close connection the apostle makes between the latter rain and the blotting out of sin. He says the refreshing is not optional but essential to the final cleansing of God's people. This agrees with the inspired metaphor. In ancient Israel, the latter rain was absolutely essential to ripen the harvest. No latter rain, no harvest. The very purpose of the latter rain is the final stage of our growth to reach maturity—our sealing by the atonement of Christ—His final blotting out of our sin.

Since this is a new thought to some and one that is controverted by others, let's look carefully now at the Levitical Day of Atonement service, comparing it to the passages in Revelation that describe the latter rain and final ministry of Christ to see what the Scriptures teach and what the practical implications are.

For easy reference, here is the law of the Day of Atonement:

And the LORD said unto Moses, Speak unto Aaron thy brother, that he come not at all times into the holy place within the veil before the mercy seat, which is upon the ark; that he die not: for I will appear in the cloud upon the mercy seat.

Thus shall Aaron come into the holy place: with a young bullock for a sin offering, and a ram for a burnt offering. He shall put on the holy linen coat, and he shall have the linen breeches upon his flesh, and shall be girded with a linen girdle, and with the linen miter shall he be attired: these are holy garments; therefore shall he wash his flesh in water, and so put them on. And he shall take of the congregation of the children of Israel two kids of the goats for a sin offering, and one ram for a burnt offering. And Aaron shall offer his bullock of the sin offering, which is for himself, and make an atonement for himself, and for his house. And he shall take the two goats, and present them before the LORD at the door of the tabernacle of the congregation.

And Aaron shall cast lots upon the two goats; one lot for the LORD, and the other lot for the scapegoat. And Aaron shall bring the goat upon which the LORD'S lot fell, and offer him for a sin offering. But the goat, on which the lot fell to be the scapegoat, shall be presented alive before the LORD, to make an atonement with him, and to let him go for a scapegoat into the wilderness. And Aaron shall bring the bullock of the sin offering, which is for himself, and shall make an atonement for himself, and for his house, and shall kill the bullock of the sin offering which is for himself: And he shall take a censer full of burning coals of fire from off the altar before the LORD, and his hands full of sweet incense beaten small, and bring it within the vail:

And he shall put the incense upon the fire before the LORD, that the cloud of the incense may cover the mercy seat that is upon the testimony, that he die not: And he shall take of the blood of the bullock, and sprinkle it with his finger upon the mercy seat eastward; and before the mercy seat shall he sprinkle of the blood with his finger seven times. Then shall he kill the goat of the sin offering, that is for the people, and bring his blood within the vail, and do with that blood as he did with the blood of the bullock, and sprinkle it upon the mercy seat, and before the mercy seat: And he shall make an atonement for the holy place, because of the uncleanness of the children of Israel, and because of their transgressions in all their sins: and so shall he do for the tabernacle of the congregation, that remaineth among them in the midst of their uncleanness. And there shall be no man in the tabernacle of the congregation when he goeth in to make an atonement in the holy place, until he come out, and have made an atonement for himself, and for his household, and for all the congregation of Israel.

And he shall go out unto the altar that is before the LORD, and make an atonement for it; and shall take of the blood of the bullock, and of the blood of the goat, and put it upon the horns of the altar round about. And he shall sprinkle of the blood upon it with his finger seven times, and cleanse it, and hallow it from the uncleanness of the children of Israel. And when he hath made an end of reconciling the holy place, and the tabernacle of the congregation, and the altar, he shall bring the live goat: And Aaron shall lay both his hands upon the head of the live goat, and confess over him all the iniquities of the children of Israel, and all their transgressions in all their sins, putting them upon the head of the goat, and shall send him away by the hand of a fit man into the wilderness. (Leviticus 16:2–21)

In the Levitical service, a national atonement was performed, and the sanctuary was cleansed in the autumn at harvest time. During the year, sins had been confessed and transferred in type to the sanctuary. The Day of Atonement pointed forward to the end of the age, when these would be blotted out and the heavenly sanctuary would be cleansed, as foretold in Daniel 8:14.

The Day of Atonement

In the Levitical service, the annual purging of sin took place in two stages: the first at the mercy seat covering the ark of the covenant containing the broken law, and the second and final stage at the golden altar of incense.

In the initial stage, the high priest first atoned for himself and his family with a bull for a sin offering. Next, he atoned for the congregation with a goat for the sins of the people. In both cases, except for the animal, the rituals were identical: The blood, representing the life of the innocent animals, was brought to the mercy seat, a symbol of the throne of God, where it was sprinkled seven times directly above the law contained within the ark, first with the blood of the bull and then with the blood of the goat. The Scriptures state that this perfect, sevenfold cleansing atoned for the entire sanctuary, both the Holy and Most Holy places (refer to verse 16).

From this divine illustration, we can see the *yearly* service was the cure or remedy for the *daily* services, which had transferred the sins of the people to the sanctuary. In the same way, at the end of time, as the ministry of Christ comes to a close, there is a final removal and blotting out of previously confessed sins. The atonement of Christ under the refreshing of His Spirit is combined with the trials and tests that reveal to God's people what is in their hearts and whether their sins have been truly confessed and forsaken. This ministry of Christ seals the person in a sacred, tender, covenant relationship with God.

During this part of the service, no one was permitted to be in either apartment of the sanctuary other than the high priest (see verse 17). Except for the tinkling of the bells on the border of the high priest's robe, the sanctuary fell silent. It was a day of judgment, and Israel was quiet and humble before the Lord, dependent on the intercessory work of one man.

This period of silence is prophetic, pointing us forward to those end-time prophecies where the court of heaven convenes, the judgment is set, and the Ancient of Days presides, holding a seven-sealed scroll in His right hand.

> As I looked, thrones were placed, and the Ancient of Days took his seat; his clothing was white as snow, and the hair of his head like pure wool; his throne was fiery flames; its wheels were burning fire. A stream of fire issued and came out from before him; a thousand thousands served him, and ten thousand times ten thousand stood before him; the court sat in judgment, and the books were opened.... And I saw in the night visions, and behold, with the clouds of heaven there came one like a son

of man, and he came to the Ancient of Days and was presented before him. And to him was given dominion and glory and a kingdom, that all peoples, nations, and languages should serve him; his dominion is an everlasting dominion, which shall not pass away, and his kingdom one that shall not be destroyed. (Daniel 7:9, 10, 13, 14, ESV)

In John's parallel vision, when the Father takes His place on the throne, scroll in hand, we have a still fuller picture. In this account, once the court is seated, the all-important question is posed: "Who is worthy to take the book and break its seals?" Silence and suspense follow while a universal search is made for one who is qualified to open the book. But no created being in heaven or earth is found worthy to take the book or even look on it (see Rev. 5:1–3).

John was so distraught by this that he cried bitter tears of anguish. No created being, none of even the most exalted and powerful of the heavenly hosts had come forward to speak or open the book. As it became painfully clear that no one had been found, John's suspense changed to anguish. This was not just a passing indisposition. We're told he "wept much" (verse 4). He understood, in some sense, that the honor of God and the destiny of His people was trembling in the balance—that humanity was doomed unless these seals were broken and the providence of God was unlocked and revealed in the final events of earth's history.

John's anguish evoked the sympathy of one of the twenty-four elders who bid him look up and take heart; the elder assured him that the Lamb had indeed prevailed to break the seals and open the book (see verses 4, 5).

At the elder's bidding, John looks, and the scene has changed: A Lion-Lamb, the Priest-King, is escorted by an angelic host before the Ancient of Days and presented before Him (see Dan. 7:13; Rev. 5:6). As the crowned Lion-Lamb takes the scroll from the Father's hand, the courts of heaven resound with praise and adoration. Then, as He breaks the first four seals, a voice of thunder summons four horsemen in succession; soon afterward, He breaks open the remaining three.

Just as on the Day of Atonement, there was a sevenfold blood cleansing of the mercy seat, a symbol of the divine throne, so there are seven seals on the scroll when the Father takes His seat on the throne of judgment. By virtue of the blood of the Lamb, these seals are broken, and the final course of earth's history unfolds before the prophet.

As in the typical service, where no one was permitted within the sanctuary for the duration of its cleansing, so in the antitype, no one except the Lion-Lamb is permitted to read the scroll and break its seals.

Only the Son of Man can unlock earth's final events and fully liberate us from the dominion of sin. Only He can inspect and cleanse the sanctuary of our souls of their defilement because only He has been tempted in all points like we are yet fully overcame. He is the one being who perfectly, mysteriously combines human nature with the divine. He alone, therefore, holds the remedy for our sin: His own blood, which has infinite power to acquit, cleanse, and transform our souls.

With the deepest interest, heaven looked on, in silent wonder, at this mediatorial work of the Lamb. His ministry reached an important milestone in 1844, when the judgment began. This is described especially in the fifth seal:

> And when he had opened the fifth seal, I saw under the altar the souls of them that were slain for the word of God, and for the testimony which they held: And they cried with a loud voice, saying, How long, O Lord, holy and true, dost thou not judge and avenge our blood on them that dwell on the earth? And white robes were given unto every one of them [they were pronounced pure and holy]; and it was said unto them, that they should rest yet for a little season, until their fellowservants and their brethren, that should be killed as they were, should be fulfilled. (Revelation 6:9–11)

Here, the dead were judged. The phrase I supplied in the passage above, "they were pronounced pure and holy," was employed by Ellen White in a letter from 1892, where she quoted this passage and then commented, "Here were scenes presented to John that were not in reality but that which would be in a period of time in the future" (*Manuscript Releases*, vol 20, p. 198).

Significantly, she placed this scene in the future, suggesting that the fifth seal marks the completion of the investigative judgment of the dead. This is where we are today. Once the dead are judged, the seismic sixth seal follows, announcing the judgment of the living.

Cleansing the Golden Altar

So far, we've looked at six of the seven seals. In the typical Day of Atonement, after the seven sprinklings on the mercy seat, the high priest exited the Most Holy place to perform the last stage: the cleansing of the golden altar. In the antitype, at the seventh and final seal, there is a second profound silence, this time for the space of about half an hour (see Rev. 8:1). Just as the first pause and silence marked the start of the sevenfold cleansing of the holy places, this one marks its completion and the start of this final phase.

In the type, this is what follows:

> And he shall go out [of the Most Holy Place] unto the [golden] altar that is before the LORD, and make an atonement for it; and shall take of the blood of the bullock, and of the blood of the goat, and put it upon the horns of the altar round about. And he shall sprinkle of the blood upon it with his finger seven times, and cleanse it, and hallow it from the uncleanness of the children of Israel. (Leviticus 16:18, 19)

The antitype of the above cleansing is found in Revelation 8. In this scene, after the half hour of silence, Christ approaches the golden altar of incense. Like in the type, He is given much incense—two nail-pierced hands full of His fragrant righteousness—to mingle with our prayers, making them aromatic and beautiful before God (see Rev. 8:2–4).

These are the prayers of those who cry and sigh between the porch and the altar for their own sins and those of God's people (see Ezek. 9:4; Joel 2:17). As a tender, attentive Father, the Lord hears those who earnestly intercede with Him for themselves and others. He encourages their perseverance and patience and then answers their petitions with His Spirit and His seal. By the virtue of His blood, Christ imparts the refreshing to them as He casts the fire of His Spirit on the earth, accompanied by supernatural "voices, and thunderings, and lightnings, and an earthquake" (Rev. 8:5; see also Ezek. 10:2, 6, 7).

Then the first five of the seven trumpets sound in quick succession. Whether these are literal, symbolic, or a combination of both is not easy to say, but they clearly contain symbolic elements. What is beyond doubt is their purpose: They are divine warnings—trumpet calls to repentance that sound globally as Christ completes the cleansing of the golden alter, pointing humanity to His work for us there:

- First trumpet: Fiery hail mingled with blood consumes all the grass and a third of the trees of the earth.

- Second trumpet: A giant burning object, the size of a mountain, is thrown into the sea, destroying a third of the ships and sea life.

- Third trumpet: A deadly "star" falls on the springs and rivers of fresh water, poisoning a third of them.

- Fourth trumpet: The sun, moon, and stars are struck so that a third of their light is obscured.

- Fifth trumpet: The bottomless pit opens, and locusts emerge that torment unrepentant humanity for five months (see Rev. 8:6–13; 9:1–12).

At the sounding of the sixth trumpet the cleansing of the golden altar is almost complete. A voice issues from its blood-cleansed horns, releasing the four angels who, until this point, have held back the four winds of strife: "And the sixth angel sounded, *and I heard a voice from the four horns of the golden altar* which is before God, Saying to the sixth angel which had the trumpet, *Loose the four angels which are bound in the great river Euphrates. And the four angels were loosed*" (Rev. 9:13–15, emphasis added).

Just as the seven seals of Revelation are symbolized by the sevenfold cleansing of the mercy seat, the seven trumpets are symbolized by the sevenfold sprinkling of the golden altar. The trumpets are the final call to us to participate in the atonement of Christ by confessing and forsaking our sins. Once the work of blotting out is complete, at the seventh trumpet, great voices in heaven proclaim, "The kingdoms of this world are become the kingdoms of our Lord, and of his Christ; and he shall reign for ever and ever," and the Father announces, "It is done" (11:19; 16:17).

> The trumpets are the final call to us to participate in the atonement of Christ by confessing and forsaking our sins.

When God makes this announcement, the dominion of sin is at an end. Evil and the devil are vanquished and the sins of God's people are forever blotted out. They are borne out of the heavenly sanctuary by Christ and placed on the head of the scapegoat, Satan, who is led into the wilderness, then to his destruction in the lake of fire. Probation for humanity has closed, and soon the Son of Man appears in the clouds. He puts his sickle to the wheat and gathers every precious grain of it into his garner (see 14:14–16).

Chapter 6

The Unfulfilled Spring Feasts

Earlier, we looked at the imminent coronation of Christ, the ignition of the seven lamps of fire, and the cleansing of the sanctuary. Let's look now at what the prophets have to say about the timing of these.

Based on sacred history, the most likely time for events of this magnitude would be at the biblical feasts. The ministry and crucifixion of Christ were foretold to the day and hour by the sacred feasts and the prophecies of Daniel 9, and the final cleansing of the sanctuary is typified in the Day of Atonement.

Until recently, many Bible believers like me have thought all the Levitical spring feasts were fulfilled by Christ: 1) His death at Passover, 2) His resurrection at Firstfruits, and 3) the outpouring of the Holy Spirit at Pentecost. However, if we scour sacred history, we find there is actually another spring feast that has never been fulfilled: the seven-day Feast of Unleavened Bread, also called "Passover week."

This week was first observed on the night the firstborn Egyptians were slain and the Hebrews began their journey to the Promised Land, but the Egyptians, the most powerful nation at that time, after letting them go, changed their minds and went after them. Their final deliverance was completed seven days later, on the last day of the feast, a Sabbath, at the drowning of Pharaoh and his army in the Red Sea. As Israel watched the Almighty fight for them that day on the far shore of the sea (remember, it was a Sabbath, a day of rest), they were filled with awe; the spirit of inspiration reverberated through the assembled nation with exultant songs of worship, adoration, and rejoicing.

When Moses and Aaron first approached Pharoah and asked him to release God's people, they said, "Thus saith the LORD God of Israel, Let my people go, that they may hold a feast unto me in the wilderness" (Exod. 5:1). If Pharaoh had complied, Israel would have celebrated the feast, yet he would have lived.

This is the only feast the Hebrews celebrated in the wilderness between Egypt and Mount Sinai. And to this day, the Jews still recite the song of Moses in their synagogues on the seventh day of Passover week and celebrate the event in their homes with feasting, singing, and dancing. The feast marked their complete deliverance and their birth as a nation. The enslaved were now totally free, beyond the sea that borders Egypt and on the first leg of their journey to the Promised Land.

In the antitype, we see a similar liberation at the start of the final march home in Revelation 14. The redeemed sing a song of rejoicing as they are about to embark on the final stage of their journey. Mark the encouraging parallel we find in Revelation 15: Like the Hebrews on the far shores of the Red Sea, the redeemed are standing on a sea of glass, and they actually sing the same song, the song of Moses. When do they sing it? Possibly on the same day it was first sung: the seventh day of Passover, a type that has yet to be fulfilled:

> And they sung as it were a new song before the throne, and before the four beasts, and the elders: and no man could learn that song but the hundred and forty and four thousand, which were redeemed from the earth.... And they sing the song of Moses the servant of God, and the song of the Lamb, saying, Great and marvelous are thy works, Lord God Almighty; just and true are thy ways, thou King of saints. Who shall not fear thee, O Lord, and glorify thy name? for thou only art holy: for all nations shall come and worship before thee; for thy judgments are made manifest. (Revelation 14:3; 15:3, 4)

Unlike the ancient liberated captives, notice above that the redeemed sing this song *before* the plagues fall. Why? Apparently, because they know what is about to happen. Like the Israelites, they have had a foretaste of the seismic judgments of God; they have seen enough of the marvelous justice and mercy of God to know where they stand prophetically and have complete confidence that, as severe as the impending plagues will be, He will execute them in infinite justice and righteousness. Through their own life experiences, they know He is worthy of profound adoration and endless praise.

The Week of Atonement

With that said, is the Feast of Unleavened Bread the only unfulfilled spring feast? Actually, no. There is one more little-known service that we'll look at now.[3]

This obscure feast is found in Ezekiel's temple vision, recorded in chapters 40–48. In the middle of the description, there is a fascinating atonement provision, a week of atonement, something new and unheard of in the Mosaic code. This service has not only never been fulfilled; it has never been observed by the Jews. Why? Because Ezekiel's temple, although similar to the ancient tabernacle, is governed by quite different laws; the building, layout, furniture, and ritual are all significantly different.

Because of these perplexing differences, for the past twenty-five centuries, the vision has been like a sealed book—an enigma—to Jews and Christians alike. However, the mystery starts to unfold when it's observed that the vision contains many elements pointing to the restoration of the Israel of God in the last days. It applies to the remnant who will understand its meaning. In my companion book, *Ezekiel's Temple*, I review how the different elements of the vision illuminate the final atonement of Christ vividly portrayed in the books of Daniel and Revelation.

One of the major differences between the Mosaic ritual and Ezekiel's temple is this new week of atonement. Although very different from the Levitical Day of Atonement, Ezekiel's service complements the Mosaic and is an important window into it.

Here, the cleansing is not just a one-day service, as in the Levitical model, but spans a full week. It starts on the first day of the first month of the Hebrew year, which is late March/early April on our calendar. The specifications of the service are as follows:

> Thus saith the Lord God; In the first month, in the first day of the month, thou shalt take a young bullock without blemish, and cleanse the sanctuary: And the priest shall take of the blood of the sin offering, and put it upon the posts of the house, and upon the four corners of the settle of the altar, and upon the posts of the gate of the inner court. And so thou shalt do the seventh day of the month for every one that erreth,

---

[3] One of the hazards of drawing attention to the biblical feast days is that some souls are naturally inclined towards making them tests of faith and reverting to the religion of the old covenant. This issue was settled at the first church council recorded in Acts 15.

and for him that is simple: so shall ye reconcile the house. (Ezekiel 45:18–20)

The atonement in Ezekiel's temple is far from unique in the ceremonial law. It is actually the norm, and the Levitical Day of Atonement is the exception. Under Levitical law, the various cleansing laws for individuals who became ceremonially unclean always spanned seven days. Also, in both services, the ordination for the priesthood spans seven days because seven is the number of completeness and perfection.

In Ezekiel's atonement liturgy (the text above), unlike the Levitical service, there is no goat, the offering for the people. Instead, only a bull, the offering of the priest, is offered on the first and seventh days. The service finds its antitype in Revelation 4–7 and 14, where the 144,000 are sealed and ordained as priest-kings (see Rev. 5, 7); and when their sealing is complete, they sing a new song, the song of Moses, offering sublime adoration and thanks to God and the Lamb who has redeemed them, the first fruits of His atoning work (see 14:1–5; 15:2–5). They stand spotless and without fault before the throne of God. And having been sealed in their foreheads, they are especially empowered to bear the everlasting gospel to the world.

Like the Day of Atonement, which cleansed the sanctuary and prepared the nation for the joyful Feast of Tabernacles, this week of atonement has the same function: preparing spiritual Israel and the royal priesthood for the antitypical passover and feast of unleavened bread.

Where, among the feasts, is the best fit for the atonement of the 144,000? I suggest it is the spring week of atonement of Ezekiel's temple because 1) the 144,000 are the first fruits, which, in Israel, were offered in the spring on the day after the Passover Sabbath, and 2) they are spotless and completely faultless, the product of the full, seven-day service.

If this is correct, it has major implications for the end-time church because it points to this atonement as especially applying to their case. The spring atonement is a potent lesson book for the remnant on how to cooperate with Christ in His intercessory work for them.

The pioneers of Adventism, by carefully studying the sanctuary and the fall feasts, understood their prophetic position, and the Lord empowered their message. The same will be true of the remnant: Those who prayerfully, intently study the sanctuary and its services will understand best the final atonement of Christ; they will "follow the Lamb whithersoever he goeth" and teach others how to do the same.

Regarding the 144,000, in 1902, Ellen White stated, "Just as soon as the people of God are sealed in their foreheads ... and prepared for the shaking, it will come. Indeed, it has begun already. The judgments of God are now upon the land, to give us warning, that we may know what is coming" (*Manuscript Releases*, vol. 10, p. 252). Notice that when the saints are sealed, the shaking immediately intensifies. Her prophecy applies uniquely to the 144,000 because, in all of Scripture, the 144,000 are the one and only vanguard group sealed by God in their foreheads (see Rev. 7: 3, 4; 14:1).

The Dedication of the Levitical Tabernacle

The original tabernacle was erected by Moses on the first day of the first month of the Hebrew year, one year after the Exodus. When it was erected, Aaron and his sons were ordained for seven days, starting on day one of the year.

As we saw earlier, the atonement service of Ezekiel's temple spans the same week. In this atonement, unlike the Levitical service, only a bull, the sin offering of a priest, is offered. This is a type of the end-time cleansing of the royal Melchizedek priesthood we see in Revelation 5:8–10, who are ordained and commissioned as priest-kings. Their ordination sets the wheels of prophecy in unstoppable motion for the final victory of the church.

Let us examine an inspired reference to this group:

> Those who eat the flesh and drink the blood of the Son of God will bring from the books of Daniel and Revelation truth that is inspired by the Holy Spirit. They will start into action forces that cannot be repressed. The lips of children will be opened to proclaim the mysteries that have been hidden from the minds of men....
>
> We are standing on the threshold of great and solemn events. Many of the prophecies are about to be fulfilled in quick succession. Every element of power is about to be set to work. Past history will be repeated; old controversies will arouse to new life, and peril will beset God's people on every side. Intensity is taking hold of the human family. It is permeating everything upon the earth.
>
> Daniel's example of prayer and confession is given for our instruction and encouragement. (White, *Letters and Manuscripts*, vol. 16, ms. 142-1901, par. 11, 15, 16)

The Tenth Day of the First Month

In the Levitical type, the Passover lamb was set aside and dedicated to God on the tenth day of the first month, four days before Passover—a fit symbol of God's acceptance of this remnant following their atonement. Historically, this was the day Israel miraculously crossed the swollen Jordan River on dry ground. That same day, the men were all circumcised, and the Lord removed the reproach of Israel. He accepted them and renewed His covenant with Israel by the sign of circumcision (see Josh. 5:9). The conquest of the Promised Land started here at the Jordan and was followed soon afterward with the siege and overthrow of Jericho.

Recall that the conquest of Jericho was accomplished by a march of seven days around the city to the sounding of trumpets, pointing to the seven trumpets of Revelation. The siege ended on the seventh day with a sevenfold march around the city, symbolic of the seven plagues and the Battle of Armageddon, when the walls of spiritual Babylon will be overthrown and that great harlot will be cast like a millstone into the sea (see Rev. 18:21).

The spring atonement in Ezekiel's temple points to the gracious protection of God during this time when Babylon is judged. In the spring week of atonement, the blood is applied to the posts of the temple and the inner court as the blood of the first Passover lambs was applied to the doorposts and lintels of the Hebrew homes, protecting the eldest from the angel of death. The Passover symbolism employed in the spring atonement telegraphs to us that this atonement occurs during a time of judgment on God's enemies and a time when His people are sheltered within His pavilion.

> **"**
> The Passover symbolism employed in the spring atonement telegraphs to us that this atonement occurs during a time of judgment on God's enemies and a time when His people are sheltered within His pavilion.
> **"**

Furthermore, in Ezekiel's temple, the Passover theme continues seven days later in the Passover week and is repeated seven months later in the fall feast, which is a second Passover service. Unlike the Levitical spring and fall feasts, which differ from each other, the Passover theme of Ezekiel's temple permeates the whole cycle of the year, indicating this temple is the type of our sanctuary in God when the shaking begins and the overflowing scourge passes through.

To recap, the spring week of atonement illuminates the ministry of Christ on behalf of the 144,000, who are the first fruits of His final mediation. In the Mosaic service and Ezekiel's temple, the priests are purified and ordained between day one and day seven of the first month.

On the tenth day, the Passover lamb was selected and set aside. On the afternoon of the fourteenth, the Passover was celebrated, and, at sundown, the seven-day Feast of Unleavened Bread began. The Feast of Firstfruits followed after the Passover Sabbath, on the second day of Unleavened Bread, a symbol, not only of Christ and those who were raised with Him at His resurrection, but also of the 144,000, the first fruits who appear with Christ on Mount Zion (see Matt. 27:53; Rev. 14:4). On the twenty-first day, the seventh day of Unleavened Bread, Israel rejoiced in the deliverance of God on the far shores of the Red Sea, a type of the rejoicing pictured in Revelation 14:1–5 and 15:2–5.

Speaking prophetically, David refers to this future Passover:

He that dwelleth in the secret place of the most High shall abide under the shadow of the Almighty. I will say of the LORD, He is my refuge and my fortress: my God; in him will I trust. Surely he shall deliver thee from the snare of the fowler, and from the noisome pestilence. He shall cover thee with his feathers, and under his wings shalt thou trust: his truth shall be thy shield and buckler. Thou shalt not be afraid for the terror by night; nor for the arrow that flieth by day; Nor for the pestilence that walketh in darkness; nor for the destruction that wasteth at noonday. A thousand shall fall at thy side, and ten thousand at thy right hand; but it shall not come nigh thee. Only with thine eyes shalt thou behold and see the reward of the wicked. Because thou hast made the LORD, which is my refuge, even the most High, thy habitation; There shall no evil befall thee, neither shall any plague come nigh thy dwelling. (Psalm 91:1–10)

Chapter 7

The Seven Thunders

And I saw another mighty angel come down from heaven, clothed with a cloud: and a rainbow was upon his head, and his face was as it were the sun, and his feet as pillars of fire: And he had in his hand a little book open: and he set his right foot upon the sea, and his left foot on the earth, And cried with a loud voice, as when a lion roareth: and when he had cried, seven thunders uttered their voices. And when the seven thunders had sounded, I was about to write, but I heard a voice from heaven saying, "Seal up what the seven thunders have said, and do not write it down."

Revelation 10:1–4

Ellen White identified the mighty angel of Revelation 10 as Christ and made the following insightful comment:

The mighty angel who instructed John was no less a personage than Jesus Christ. Setting His right foot on the sea, and His left upon the dry land, shows the part which He is acting in the closing scenes of the great controversy with Satan. This position denotes His supreme power and authority over the whole earth.... He is to show the power and authority of His voice to those who have united with Satan to oppose the truth. (White, *The SDA Bible Commentary*, vol. 7, p. 971)

How does Christ show His power and authority over the world? By His overruling providences and judgments that allow the truth of the gospel to radiate in all directions from the seven blazing lamps of fire, the final church. Through it, a true knowledge of God blankets the earth as the waters cover the sea, imparting to humanity the last invitation to the wedding—the last message of mercy (see Hab. 2:14).

Notice carefully that these seven blazing lamps are fueled by the oil of the two olive trees, God's two anointed, and kindled by the coals of fire from the golden altar of Christ's intercession (see Zech. 4:14; Isa. 6:6; Rev. 8:5). The seven thunders therefore occur during the latter rain.

Historically, the seven thunders of Revelation 10 are connected to the Millerites, the pioneers of Adventism, and the bittersweet little book. After the disappointment of 1844, Adventists did not reach any consensus regarding them. Some thought perhaps the seven thunders were fulfilled in the Millerite movement, but there were no seven events that matched up. To their credit, the early Adventists acknowledged this. A little later, other Adventists, such as Uriah Smith, believed the thunders were future and still sealed.

However, Ellen White took a somewhat different approach. She, like Smith, also placed them in the future, but at the same time, she told how they would be unsealed and linked them to when the three angels' messages are repeated under the latter rain:

> After these seven thunders uttered their voices, the injunction comes to John as to Daniel in regard to the little book: "Seal up those things which the seven thunders uttered." *These relate to future events which will be disclosed in their order. Daniel shall stand in his lot at the end of the days.* John sees the little book unsealed. Then Daniel's prophecies have their proper place in the first, second, and third angels' messages to be given to the world. (White, *The SDA Bible Commentary*, vol. 7, p. 971, emphasis added)

The emphasized sentences indicate that the thunders will be unsealed by the prophecies of the little book of Daniel and this occurs at "the end of days." This agrees with Daniel 12:4. Like John, Daniel was also told to seal up the book until the time of the end: "But you, Daniel, shut up the words and seal the book, *until the time of the end.* Many shall run to and fro, and knowledge [of those prophecies that have been sealed] shall increase" (emphasis added).

With this in mind, let me ask, Are we living in "the time of the end"? If so, isn't it time to do what the angel says: eat the little book (because it is *open* in the hand of the angel), study the prophecies, and run "to and fro," sharing and comparing our findings in order to enhance our collective understanding (see Rev. 10:8, 9)? Isn't it time to obey the divine direction so we're qualified to fulfill the commission of the remnant to rise and "prophesy again" (see verse 11; 11:1)? In keeping with that direction, I'm going to share my view of the seven thunders now.

Ellen White said the thunders are "future events" that "will be disclosed in their order." That's both exciting and comforting because it assures us that, as each thunder utters its voice, we'll know with confidence and precision where we stand prophetically in these turbulent times. These seven utterances will be an anchor and guide for us.

One clue to their meaning is their origin: It is the voice of the mighty angel, roaring like a lion that causes the seven thunders to sound throughout the earth. "And *he* cried with a loud voice, as when a lion roareth: and when he had cried, seven thunders uttered their voices" (10:3).

In nature, thunder and lightning announce a storm. In the spiritual world, God's thunderous voice announces the latter rains:

> The voice of thy thunder was in the heaven: the lightnings lightened the world: the earth trembled and shook. The clouds poured out water: the skies sent out a sound: thine arrows also went abroad.... Thou leddest thy people like a flock. (Psalm 77:18, 17, 20)

> Give unto the LORD, O ye mighty, give unto the LORD glory and strength. Give unto the LORD the glory due unto his name; worship the LORD in the beauty of holiness. The voice of the LORD is upon the waters: the God of glory thundereth: the LORD is upon many waters. The voice of the LORD is powerful; the voice of the LORD is full of majesty.... and in his temple doth every one speak of his glory. The LORD sitteth upon the flood; yea, the LORD sitteth King for ever. The LORD will give strength unto his people; the LORD will bless his people with peace. (Psalm 29:2–4, 9–11)

The thunders are revealed in the little book, which is open to believers, but sealed to unbelievers. "None of the wicked will understand" Daniel's prophecies (Dan. 12:10).

Now, regarding the first thunder, my view is that this event is the final coronation of Christ that brings the latter rain because it is accompanied by supernatural thunder.

> After this I looked, and, behold, a door was opened in heaven: and the first voice which I heard was as it were of a trumpet talking with me; which said, Come up hither, and I will shew thee things which must

be hereafter. And immediately I was in the spirit: and, behold, a throne was set in heaven, and one sat on the throne. And round about the throne were four and twenty seats: *And out of the throne proceeded lightnings and thunderings and voices: and there were seven lamps of fire burning before the throne, which are the seven Spirits of God.* (Revelation 4:1–5, emphasis added)

This event is followed soon afterward by the opening of the first four seals, which are announced with a voice of thunder. These appear to be the second thunder. At the sixth seal, the Lord roars from Zion, and the earth is mightily shaken. I suggest this is the third thunder. Then further on, there are three more events where supernatural "lightenings, thunderings and voices" issue from the throne of God (see Rev. 8:5; 11:19; 16:17, 18). Each of these appears to be a thunder. Between Revelation 8:5 and 11:19, the voice of God issues from the four horns of the golden alter, which I suggest is the fifth thunder.

To summarize, we can account for all seven thunders by reading the little open book as follows:

- First thunder: The supernatural thunders at the coronation of Christ—"And immediately I was in the spirit: and, behold, a throne was set in heaven, and one sat on the throne.... *And out of the throne proceeded lightnings and thunderings and voices:* and there were seven lamps of fire burning before the throne, which are the seven Spirits of God.... The four and twenty elders ... cast their crowns before the throne, saying, Thou art worthy, O Lord, to receive glory and honour and power" (Rev. 4:2, 5, 10, 11).

- Second thunder: The announcement from heaven of the first four seals—"And I saw when the Lamb opened one of the seals, *and I heard, as it were the noise of thunder*, one of the four beasts saying, Come and see" (6:1, ESV).

- Third thunder: The thunderous earthquake of the sixth seal (Large earthquakes are often preceded by loud, hoarse, subterranean thunder)—"And I beheld when he had opened the sixth seal, *and, lo, there was a great earthquake*; and the sun became black as sackcloth of hair, and the moon became as blood; And the stars of heaven fell unto the earth, even as a fig tree casteth her untimely figs, when she is shaken of a mighty wind" (verses 12, 13, emphasis added).

- Fourth thunder: The supernatural thunders of the seventh seal—"And another angel came and stood at the altar, having a golden censer; and there was given unto him much incense, that he should offer it with the prayers of all saints upon the golden altar which was before the throne. And the angel took the censer, and filled it with fire of the altar, and cast it into the earth: *and there were voices, and thunderings, and lightnings, and an earthquake*" (8:1, 3, 5).

- Fifth thunder: The thunderous voice of God from the golden altar—"And the sixth angel sounded, and *I heard a voice from the four horns of the golden altar which is before God,* Saying to the sixth angel which had the trumpet, Loose the four angels which are bound in the great river Euphrates" (9:13, 14).

- Sixth thunder: The supernatural thunders at the opening of the temple in heaven: "And the temple of God was opened in heaven, and there was seen in his temple the ark of his testament: *and there were lightnings, and voices, and thunderings, and an earthquake,* and great hail" (11:19).

- Seventh thunder: when the Lord announces the end of human history—"And the seventh angel poured out his vial into the air; *and there came a great voice out of the temple of heaven, from the throne, saying, It is done. And there were voices, and thunders, and lightnings*; and there was a great earthquake, such as was not since men were upon the earth, so mighty an earthquake, [and] so great" (16:17, 18, emphasis added).

Chapter 8

The Sixth Seal and the Signs of the End

The second great awakening of the early 1800s was a grassroots revival as people came under the conviction of the near return of Christ. Among the most persuasive evidence of Christ's advent were three harbingers: the Great Lisbon earthquake of 1755, the mysterious dark day of New England in 1780, and the "falling of the stars," visible across North America in 1833, which was perhaps the most spectacular meteorite shower ever witnessed.

These three events were widely viewed in early-nineteenth-century America as a fulfillment of the sixth seal: "And I beheld when he had opened the sixth seal, and, lo, there was a great earthquake; and the sun became black as sackcloth of hair, and the moon became as blood; And the stars of heaven fell unto the earth, even as a fig tree casteth her untimely figs, when she is shaken of a mighty wind" (Rev. 6:12, 13).

The first of these signs, the Great Lisbon earthquake, had a global impact physically, economically, and socially. In terms of its physical impact, modern seismologists estimate it at 8.4. The tsunami that was generated off the coast of Portugal radiated in all directions across the Atlantic, causing damage in England and Ireland in the north, Spain and Morocco in the south, and as far away as the Caribbean.

Casualties from the earthquake and tsunami are estimated at 80,000. Eighty-five percent of the buildings in Lisbon were destroyed, and there was large-scale destruction to the south in Portugal, Spain, and Morocco, as well as along the coast.

The earthquake had wide-ranging effects on the lives of the populace and intelligentsia [and this was true not only of Portugal but of much of western Europe]. The earthquake had struck on an important religious holiday [All Saints Day] and had destroyed almost every important church in the city, causing anxiety and confusion amongst the citizens of a staunch and devout Roman Catholic country. Theologians and philosophers focused and speculated on the religious cause and message, seeing the earthquake as a manifestation of divine judgment.[4]

Similarly, the dark day of 1780 and the "falling of the stars" in 1833 were also events that made a vivid impression on the collective mind of youthful America and helped prepare hearts for the reception of the gospel in the second great awakening (See Appendix C for detailed descriptions of these).

However, these events, now two centuries in the past, have been largely forgotten. Since the events of the sixth seal are truly harbingers of the return of Christ, we ought to expect they will be fulfilled again. Most conservative Christians already expect this. In contrast, Adventists remain skeptical because in Adventist teaching, the time of the end began in 1798.

> However, these events, now two centuries in the past, have been largely forgotten. Since the events of the sixth seal are truly harbingers of the return of Christ, we ought to expect they will be fulfilled again. Most conservative Christians already expect this. In contrast, Adventists remain skeptical because in Adventist teaching, the time of the end began in 1798.

Something of which many Adventists are unaware is that Ellen White said similar events would be repeated. The following fascinating quote contains the words that she uttered and were recorded by those present while she was in vision in 1849:

Time of trouble, it will come right early. *The signs shall be reacted over again*; the day and hour will then be known. The sea will boil like a pot. Their faces will then shine like Moses'. He appears in the east; His sword girded on His thigh. Then deliverance comes, perfect and entire,

---

[4] "1755 Lisbon earthquake," Wikimedia Foundation, last modified June 14, 2023, https://en.wikipedia.org/wiki/1755_Lisbon_earthquake

and God's people will be caught up on the white cloud. (White, *The Ellen G. White Letters and Manuscripts*, vol. 1, p. 179)

The signs that "shall be reacted over again" is a reference to the harbingers of the sixth seal. I take her vision statements to mean these will be repeated at or shortly after the beginning of the time of trouble. The purpose of these signs is to awaken the sleeping virgins who trim their lamps and go out to welcome the Bridegroom. They apparently are components of the "overwhelming surprise."

Chapter 9

The Great San Francisco Earthquake[5]

In the spring of 1906, two weeks after the Great San Francisco earthquake, Ellen White was on her way back home to the Napa Valley. Since the city was enroute to her home, she stopped there and surveyed the damage. She described what she saw as follows:

> Yesterday, on our way home from Mountain View, we stopped to take a view of the destruction in San Francisco. Notwithstanding some of the buildings were of the most stable kind and were supposed to be proof against disaster, the city is a ruin. In some places the buildings are sunken into the ground. This city presents a most powerful picture of the inefficiency of human devising and human skill to withstand the carrying out of the Lord's mandate. (White, *Manuscript Releases*, vol. 21, p. 91)

As providence would have it, on that day, White became one of the many witnesses to the great disaster. There is nothing unusual in her narrative so far, but tucked within it, two paragraphs later, she made a clearly prophetic application of the significance of that event more than a century in the past: "Let all who would understand the meaning of these things read the eleventh chapter of Revelation. Read every verse, and learn the things that are yet to take place in the cities. Read also the scenes portrayed in the eighteenth chapter of the same book" (*Ibid.*).

---

[5] This chapter, because of its importance, was also published in the companion book, *Ezekiel's Temple*. It is adapted and included here.

Figure 5: The Great San Francisco Earthquake of 1906

According to White, there is a divine connection between this, the deadliest and costliest natural calamity to strike the west coast of America,[6] and Revelation 11 and 18. Speaking specifically of chapter 11, she said, "Read every verse and learn the things that are yet to take place in the cities." She ominously linked this chapter to the Great San Francisco earthquake. Let's consider now the beginning of Revelation 11, which gives us the context of the connection between the two: "And there was given me a reed like unto a rod: and the angel stood, saying, Rise, and measure the temple of God, and the altar, and them that worship therein" (verse 1).

"Rise, and measure the temple of God." Intuitively, we know what that means: The house (or temple) of God, the church, is being measured judged. This text is telling us "the time is come that judgment must begin at the house of God" (1 Peter 4:17). This is the same time to which Revelation 14:6 refers when "the hour of His judgment is come." The world—the nations and especially the church—are all arraigned before the bar of God. When? Judgment "is come," so the "when" would be now, and this time of judgment has been here since 1844.

Let's keep reading:

> And I will give power unto my two witnesses, and they shall prophesy a thousand two hundred and threescore days, clothed in sackcloth....

---

[6] See https://en.wikipedia.org/wiki/List_of_disasters_in_the_United_States

And if any man will hurt them, fire proceedeth out of their mouth, and devoureth their enemies: and if any man will hurt them, he must in this manner be killed.... And when they shall have finished their testimony, the beast that ascendeth out of the bottomless pit shall make war against them, and shall overcome them, and kill them. And their dead bodies shall lie in the street of *the great city*, which spiritually is called Sodom and Egypt, where also our Lord was crucified. (Revelation 11:3, 5, 7, 8, emphasis added)

The Great City

The "great city" of Revelation 11:8, where the two witnesses are slain, is spiritually called "Sodom and Egypt." On June 26, 2015, the Supreme Court of the United States issued its landmark decision on same-sex marriage.[7] And in late 2022, Congress essentially codified the court's decision into federal law in the "Respect for Marriage Act." Although the overall reaction of evangelical Americans was unfavorable, their response was, with few exceptions, alarmingly weak. Because their muteness almost amounted to mutiny, I felt impelled to write the following letter to my senator, Joe Manchin (West Virginia), currently one of the most respected and powerful leaders on Capitol Hill, on December 30, 2022:

> Dear Senator Manchin:
>
> ...
>
> I want to draw your attention to a 12 minute video released earlier this month by Jonathon Cahn addressed to President Joe Biden about his signing into law the "Respect for Marriage Act". Here is a link: https://www.youtube.com/watch?v=MqCdG-TEtvI&list=WL&index=1
>
> I hope you'll watch the video because what Cahn says to the President also applies to those who passed the bill into law. This was a national act of defiance against the government of God and his word. It was also a prophetic fulfillment of Old and New Testament scripture: Of Daniel 7 which refers to a power that thinks to change times and laws; and of Revelation 11 where the Two Witnesses of God are slain in the streets of Sodom and Egypt. I recommend and urge you to prayerfully read both of those chapters.

---

[7] Obergefell v. Hodges, 576 U.S., 135 S. Ct. 2584 (2015)

There is a reason for all divine laws: They are for our good individually and collectively. If we love those who are misguided on sexual morality we will kindly show them the path of life. I've looked hopefully to you as someone who thinks for himself and is prepared to not compromise on the principles that undergird society. Your voting in favor of this was a major victory for those who want to upend American morality, liberty and freedom of conscience. The price to us as a nation for our rebellion against God can't be overstated. I'd urge you to read and prayerfully study Deuteronomy 32 and note especially verses 32 to 47.

I understand that the pressures on you are tremendous and I want you to know you're in my prayers. We're at a time when it's not safe or wise to follow the crowd. We've seen what happens when the truth and real science are replaced with half truths and pseudo-science during the Covid pandemic. May the Lord have mercy on us to listen to the still small voice of His Spirit before we completely turn a deaf ear to Him.

Spiritual Babylon

Regarding the identity of the harlot Babylon, that great city where the witnesses are slain, a woman in Scripture is often employed as a symbol of the church; In Revelation, there is an adulterous woman—an apostate church—and a pure woman—the faithful people of God. To the extent that the unfaithful churches of the West—Europe, North America, New Zealand, and Australia—have turned from the Word of God and have thought to change it in regard to the Ten Commandments, particularly the Sabbath and marriage, the twin institutions established by God in Eden, they have become Babylon—the harlot—"that great city."

It's significant that the head of the largest of these institutions, Pope Frances, has recently signaled his endorsement of same-sex unions while at the same time denigrating Christian fundamentalists—those who take the Word of God as it reads. His hostility for evangelicals is, at

> To the extent that the unfaithful churches of the West—Europe, North America, New Zealand, and Australia—have turned from the Word of God and have thought to change it in regard to the Ten Commandments, particularly the Sabbath and marriage, the twin institutions established by God in Eden, they have become Babylon—the harlot—"that great city."

its root, hostility towards the two witnesses—the Word. They are in his crosshairs. The prophecy says the forces of apostasy will confederate to forge an apparently invincible global world order, depicted as the image of the beast, which all must worship or be killed (see Rev. 13).

Babylon, as she tightens her grip on the consciences of humanity, uses all the means of coercion that she can muster, including false accusations of disloyalty and treason, the very things of which she herself is guilty before God. However, she does not relent in the face of sacred history. Ancient Babylon, Sodom, and Egypt stand as lessons of the consequences of warring against God and flouting His Word.

With that said, what exactly is Revelation 11 telling us today? The two witnesses are sounding the warning: "Be prepared! The scenes of the Great San Francisco earthquake of 1906 and the social convulsions of Revolutionary France, the twin Sodoms[8] of modern history, are about to be repeated in America's cities, and for the same reason: People have made void the Word of God." And would it be unreasonable to expect that when the divine measuring rod of Revelation 11 is produced again and "that great city" comes under the judgment of God, it will be announced in the same way: a series of seismic events will shake Mystery Babylon and the world to the core?

---

[8] As in eighteenth-century Revolutionary France, San Francisco has for many years been at the forefront of the movement to overthrow biblical morality and the definition of marriage. Regarding the causes of the social convulsions and anarchy that decimated France for several years during its revolutionary period, see chapter 15 of *The Great Controversy*, by Ellen White.

Chapter 10

Revelation's Earthquakes

Earlier, we saw that the Great San Francisco earthquake was a foreshadowing of the future fulfillment of Revelation 11. In the Bible's final book, there are at least three end-time earthquakes we need to explore: The first earthquake occurs within the sixth seal; the second earthquake, within the seventh seal; and the third earthquake, within the seventh plague.

Revelation is clearly a book of symbols, so in the case of earthquakes these could well be symbolic of global-scale wars, international social chaos, etc. However, wherever a literal interpretation of Scripture is plausible, it is the first one that should be considered. We'll look at that now.

Some Christians teach that the earthquake of the sixth seal was the Great Lisbon earthquake of 1755, the largest to strike western Europe in the last five centuries. As noted earlier, it destroyed 85 percent of that city, and the tsunami generated caused extensive damage on two continents. While this is a valid application, because the quake of the sixth seal occurs shortly before Christ returns, it also has a future application. Ellen White repeatedly confirmed this. In addition, the Lisbon quake, as overwhelming as it was, does not meet all the particulars of the sixth seal. For example, it was not accompanied by a revelation of divine majesty that caused the terror and flight of the wicked.

The earthquake of the sixth seal is especially important because it is the initial great wake-up call to humanity, and, as we'll see in the next chapter, it occurs shortly before the latter rain.

And I beheld when he had opened the sixth seal, and, lo, there was a great earthquake; and the sun became black as sackcloth of hair, and the moon became as blood; And the stars of heaven fell unto the earth, even as a fig tree casteth her untimely figs, when she is shaken of a mighty wind.... And the kings of the earth, and the great men, and the rich men, and the chief captains, and the mighty men, and every bondman, and every free man, hid themselves in the dens and in the rocks of the mountains; And said to the mountains and rocks, Fall on us, and hide us from the face of him that sitteth on the throne, and from the wrath of the Lamb: For the great day of his wrath is come; and who shall be able to stand? (Revelation 6:12, 13, 15–17)

In the sixth seal, we have a graphic picture of abject terror among every class of people on earth. To get a clearer understanding of what this kind of overpowering revelation entails, we'll look now at two instances in Scripture where this occurred.

At the beginning of His ministry, Christ announced His mission and displayed His credentials by cleansing the temple. As He rose to cleanse it, the corrupt leaders and priests were seized with terror, realizing they were in the presence of a divine, holy Being.[iii] By this act, Christ gave the Jews unmistakable evidence of His divinity. I suggest He will do this again in the sixth seal when He arises to shake the earth, revealing His majesty again briefly, especially to unfaithful shepherds. And the results will be the same: These pastors and leaders will again cower and flee in terror.

And they shall go into the holes of the rocks, and into the caves of the earth, for fear of the LORD, and for the glory of his majesty, when he ariseth to shake terribly the earth. In that day a man shall cast his idols of silver, and his idols of gold, which they made *each one* for himself to worship, to the moles and to the bats; To go into the clefts of the rocks, and into the tops of the ragged rocks, for fear of the LORD, and for the glory of his majesty, when he ariseth to shake terribly the earth. (Isaiah 2:19–21)

Therefore I will shake the heavens, and the earth shall remove out of her place, in the wrath of the LORD of hosts, and in the day of his fierce anger. (Isaiah 13:13)

Whose voice then shook the earth: but now he hath promised, saying, Yet once more I shake not the earth only, but also heaven. And this word, Yet once more, signifieth the removing of those things that are shaken, as of things that are made, that those things which cannot be shaken may remain. (Hebrews 12:26, 27).

In the Old Testament, God gave a similar revelation of His majesty, and the wicked fled before Him in this case as well. Amos recounted that two years before a great earthquake, God put Israel on notice that He was about to roar from Zion:

The words of Amos, who was among the herdmen of Tekoa, which he saw concerning Israel in the days of Uzziah king of Judah, and in the days of Jeroboam the son of Joash king of Israel, two years before the earthquake. And he said, The LORD will roar from Zion, and utter his voice from Jerusalem; and the habitations of the shepherds shall mourn, and the top of Carmel shall wither. (Amos 1:1, 2)

This earthquake is the same one in Zechariah 14:5 before which the nation fled. I suggest it is also the same as the one in Isaiah's vision, when the posts of the temple were moved, and God asked, "Who will go for us?" Isaiah volunteered to bear God's message, and his lips were anointed with a coal from the altar (see Isa. 6:4–8). He is a type of the remnant who are shaken awake by this marker event who arise and "prophesy again." Like Isaiah, they were already commissioned beforehand with a prophetic mandate, but at this revelation of divine majesty, they keenly sense their undone condition, are humbled in God's presence, and trim their lamps to proclaim the good news. "Behold the bridegroom cometh, go ye out to meet him!" (Matt. 25:6).

In the days of Amos, the vast majority of the Jews fled from the earthquake. Why *would* they and how *could* they flee? According to Jewish tradition, this earthquake occurred when King Uzziah presumptuously went in to burn incense before God, something forbidden by the law and punishable by death. This was the case in the rebellion of Korah, Dathan, and Abiram, who were slain when they, not being priests, also presumed to offer incense before God (see 2 Chron. 26:16; Num. 16:1–40). In that case, there was also an earthquake of sorts. The ground opened and swallowed them and their families (see Num. 16:28–37).

Flavius Josephus also recorded the earthquake of Amos' time: "By [the earthquake] half of a mountain was removed and carried to a plain four furlongs off; and it spoiled the king's [Uzziah's] gardens" (*Antiquities of the*

Jews, vol. 9, p. 225). The people fled Jerusalem because God showed His displeasure at them for their wickedness and their king's presumption. God roared from Zion, and they fled from His presence. I suggest this is what God will do again at the opening of the sixth seal. He will roar from Zion and, like the Jews did, the unfaithful shepherds will run to hide from the face of Christ.

Notice in both of the above examples that the divine revelation was limited primarily to the unfaithful leaders of God's people, and in both cases, the revelation issued from Jerusalem: at Mount Zion in the days of Amos and at the Temple Mount in the days of Christ. The Old Testament prophets place the final roar of the Lord in the same location, but keep in mind that at the end, spiritual Jerusalem is the capital of spiritual Israel: those who have been entrusted with the greatest light.

Christ said, "To whom much is given, much will be required" (Luke 12:48). While the following prophecy may well apply to literal as well as spiritual Jerusalem, the principle of proportionate responsibility applies in all cases. Because Adventists have had greater light than others, they will be held accountable proportionately.

> I will also gather all nations, and will bring them down into the valley of Jehoshaphat, and will plead with them there for my people and for my heritage Israel, whom they have scattered among the nations, and parted my land.... Put ye in the sickle, for the harvest is ripe: come, get you down; for the press is full, the fats overflow; for their wickedness is great. Multitudes, multitudes in the valley of decision: for the day of the LORD is near in the valley of decision. The sun and the moon shall be darkened, and the stars shall withdraw their shining. *The LORD also shall roar out of Zion*, and utter his voice from Jerusalem; and the heavens and the earth shall shake: but the LORD will be the hope of his people, and the strength of the children of Israel.... And it shall come to pass in that day, that the mountains shall drop down new wine, and the hills shall flow with milk, and all the rivers of Judah shall flow with waters, and a fountain shall come forth of the house of the LORD, and shall water the valley of Shittim. Egypt shall be a desolation, and Edom shall be a desolate wilderness, for the violence against the children of Judah, because they have shed innocent blood in their land. But Judah shall dwell for ever, and Jerusalem from generation to generation. For I will cleanse their blood that I have not cleansed: for the LORD dwelleth in Zion. (Joel 3:2, 13–16, 18–21, emphasis added)

The Shaking Brings Atonement

Fundamentalist Christians generally speak of the shaking in terms of judgment, but the shaking described above not only brings judgment on the wicked but also atonement to God's people at the outpouring of the Spirit. A fountain of grace "shall come forth of the house of the Lord," "for I will cleanse their blood that I have not cleansed: for the LORD dwelleth in Zion." What an awesome God we serve!

While the shaking will harden the hearts of unbelievers, it will soften those of believers, and God will be a pillar of fire and cloud to the righteous, granting them liberty and victory.

To summarize, the opening of the sixth seal is signaled by a large earthquake and may be accompanied by a brief revelation of divine majesty that will be a temporary terror to most. It marks the start of the shaking and sets the stage for the latter rain. The second earthquake (of the seventh seal) may not be destructive like the first. It is part of the supernatural signs that accompany the coronation of Christ and the latter rain. The third earthquake (of the seventh plague) marks the close of human probation; it is global and accompanied by great hail, the likes of which has never been seen. This is the most terrible earthquake in human history—the one that completes the judgment of Babylon, annihilating her.

> *The opening of the sixth seal is signaled by a large earthquake and may be accompanied by a brief revelation of divine majesty that will be a temporary terror to most. It marks the start of the shaking and sets the stage for the latter rain.*

> And the seventh angel poured out his vial into the air; and there came *a great voice out of the temple of heaven, from the throne, saying, It is done.* And there were voices, and thunders, and lightnings; and there was *a great earthquake,* such as was not since men were upon the earth, so mighty an earthquake, and so great. And the great city was divided into three parts, and the cities of the nations fell: and great Babylon came in remembrance before God, to give unto her the cup of the wine of the fierceness of his wrath. (Revelation 16:17–19, emphasis added)

Notice this final earthquake, like the second, is accompanied by supernatural voices, thunder, and lightning. It is the big one.

Chapter 11

New York City and 9/11

Where do we stand prophetically now? We are in a sealing time when Christ is finishing His work of atonement for us. This is the calm before the storm:

After this I saw four angels standing at the four corners of the earth, holding the four winds of the earth, that no wind should blow on the earth, or on the sea, or upon any tree. And I saw another angel ascend from the sunrising, having the seal of the living God: and he cried with a great voice to the four angels to whom it was given to hurt the earth and the sea, saying, Hurt not the earth, neither the sea, nor the trees, till we shall have sealed the servants of our God on their foreheads. And I heard the number of them that were sealed, a hundred and forty and four thousand, sealed out of every tribe of the children of Israel. (Revelation 7:1–4).

The following quote on the sealing helps explain the above scripture:

In the night I was, I thought, in a room but not in my own house. I was in a city, where I knew not, and I heard explosion after explosion. I rose up quickly in bed, and saw from my window large balls of fire. Jetting out were sparks, in the form of arrows, and buildings were being consumed, and in a very few minutes *the entire block of buildings* was falling and the screeching and mournful groans came distinctly to my ears. I cried out, in my raised position, to learn what was happening: Where am I? And where are our family circle? *Then I awoke.* But I could not tell where I was for I was in another place than home. I said, Oh

Lord, where am I and what shall I do? It was a voice that spoke, "Be not afraid. Nothing shall harm you."

I was instructed that destruction hath gone forth upon cities. The word of the Lord will be fulfilled. Isaiah 29:19–24 was repeated. I dared not move, not knowing where I was. I cried unto the Lord, What does it mean? *These representations of destruction were repeated.* (White, *Manuscript Releases*, vol. 11, p. 361, emphasis added)

In the above vision, White saw an "entire block" of buildings fall, which is what happened in New York on September 11, 2001. The World Trade Center (WTC) complex was made up of seven buildings, four of them occupying the same block as the Twin Towers, for a total of six buildings on the WTC block and a seventh across the street on an adjoining city block (see the map below). In addition to the Twin Towers, all five of the other buildings of the WTC complex were destroyed. While surrounding buildings on adjacent blocks also suffered serious damage, only one was destroyed: WTC 7, a forty-seven-story tower that was part of the complex.

However, the ominous part of the vision is the dual repetition. The scene of destruction was repeated twice: once while she was asleep and once after she awoke. What is the significance? Notice the warning the Lord gives connected to the vision:

In scenes I have represented that which will be; but warn My people to cease from putting their trust in men who are not obedient to my warnings and who despise My reproof, for the day of the Lord is right upon the world when evidence shall be made sure. Those who have followed the voices that would turn things upside down will themselves be turned where they cannot see, but will be as blind men. (White, *Manuscript Releases*, vol. 11, p. 361)

What does God mean by telling us "for the day of the Lord is right upon the world when the evidence will be made sure"? Isn't He pointing to a future crisis of such large-scale destruction that it will leave no doubt that judgment day has arrived?

There's a similar curious interlude and repetition that occurs in a much earlier vision. In this vision, Ellen White was given the first part of it at the beginning of the Sabbath—Friday evening, January 5, 1849. In this part, she asked for an explanation of the meaning of the angel who flies to the four others with something in his hand he is waving vigorously up and

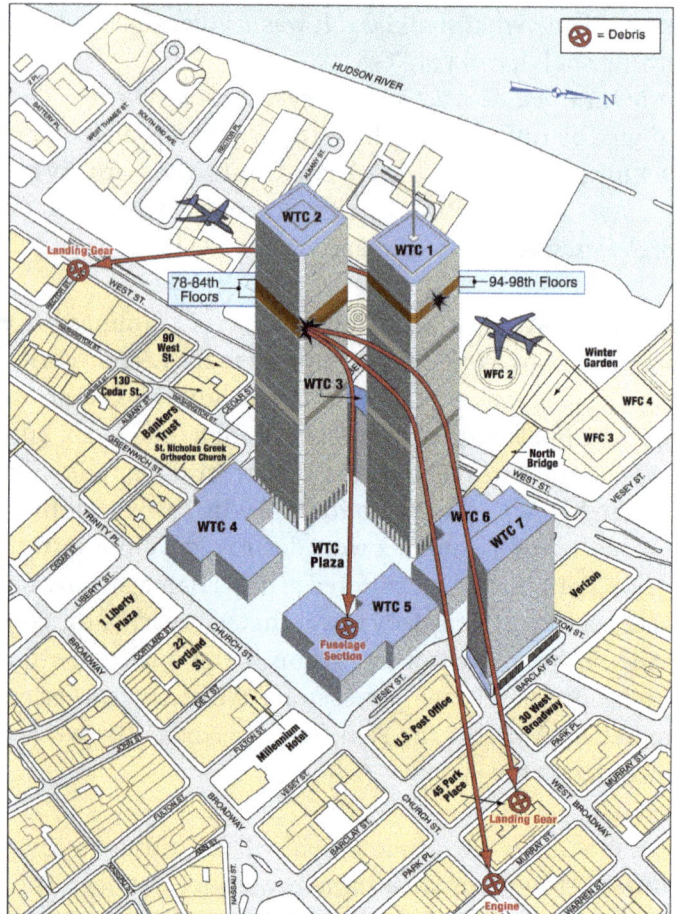

Figure 6: Government Map of the World Trade Center Attack

down, but she is told to wait—that she'll get more information shortly. On Sabbath afternoon of the following day, she was taken into vision again, and the explanation was given:

> At the commencement of the holy Sabbath, Jan. 5, 1849 [Friday evening], we engaged in prayer with Brother Belden's family at Rocky Hill, Conn., and the Holy Ghost fell upon us. I was taken off in vision to the most holy place, where I saw Jesus still interceding for Israel....
>
> I saw that the four angels would hold the four winds until Jesus' work [of sealing] was done in the sanctuary, and then will come the seven last plagues....
>
> Then my attending angel directed me to the city again, where I saw four angels winging their way to the gate of the city. They were just

presenting the golden card to the angel at the gate, when I saw another angel flying swiftly from the direction of the most excellent glory, and crying with a loud voice to the other angels, and waving something up and down in his hand. **I asked my attending angel for an explanation of what I saw. He told me that I could see no more then, but he would shortly show me what those things that I then saw meant.**

Sabbath afternoon one of our number was sick, and requested prayers that he might be healed. We all united in applying to the Physician who never lost a case, and while healing power came down, and the sick was healed, the Spirit fell upon me, and I was taken off in vision.

I saw four angels who had a work to do on the earth, and were on their way to accomplish it. Jesus was clothed with priestly garments. He gazed in pity on the remnant, then raised His hands, and with a voice of deep pity cried, "*My blood, Father, My blood! My blood! My blood!*" Then I saw an exceeding bright light come from God, who sat upon the great white throne, and was shed all about Jesus. Then I saw an angel with a commission from Jesus, swiftly flying to the four angels who had a work to do in the earth, and waving something up and down in his hand, and crying with a loud voice, "*Hold! hold! hold! hold!* until the servants of God are sealed in their foreheads."

I asked my accompanying angel the meaning of what I heard, and what the four angels were about to do. He said to me that it was God that restrained the powers, and that He gave His angels charge over things on the earth; that the four angels had power from God to hold the four winds, and that they were about to let them go; **but while their hands were loosening, and the four winds were about to blow, the merciful eye of Jesus gazed on the remnant that were not sealed, and He raised His hands to the Father, and pleaded with Him that He had spilled His blood for them. Then another angel was commissioned to fly swiftly to the four angels, and bid them hold, until the servants of God were sealed with the seal of the living God in their foreheads**. (White, *Life Sketches of Ellen G. White*, pp. 116–119, bold emphasis added)

The parallel to the interlude in the 1906 vision of falling buildings suggests that on 9/11, the winds of strife were held back and the final sealing of God's people began. What the angel was waiving up and down in his hand was the seal of God that some of God's people had not received.

> **We should cooperate in the atoning work of Christ by prayer, close self-examination, and active service for Him in good works and spreading the gospel.**

If that's so, we should cooperate in the atoning work of Christ by prayer, close self-examination, and active service for Him in good works and spreading the gospel.

Here are some more weighty prophetic statements regarding the times in which we're living and the approach of the latter rain and Armageddon:

> More and more, as the days go by, it is becoming apparent that God's judgments are in the world. In fire and flood and earthquake He is warning the inhabitants of this earth of His near approach. The time is nearing when the great crisis in the history of the world will have come, when every movement in the government of God will be watched with intense interest and inexpressible apprehension. In quick succession the judgments of God will follow one another—fire and flood and earthquake, with war and bloodshed.
>
> Oh, that the people might know the time of their visitation! There are many who have not yet heard the testing truth for this time. There are many with whom the Spirit of God is striving. *The time of God's destructive judgments is the time of mercy for those who have had no opportunity to learn what is truth. Tenderly will the Lord look upon them. His heart of mercy is touched; His hand is still stretched out to save, while the door is closed to those who would not enter.*
>
> The mercy of God is shown in His long forbearance. He is holding back His judgments, waiting for the message of warning to be sounded to all. Oh, if our people would feel as they should the responsibility resting upon them to give the last message of mercy to the world, what a wonderful work would be done!
>
> Behold the cities, and their need of the gospel! The need of earnest laborers among the multitudes of the cities has been kept before me for more than twenty years. Who are carrying a burden for the large cities? A few have felt the burden, but in comparison with the great need and the many opportunities but little attention has been given to this work. (White, *Testimonies for the Church*, vol. 9, p. 97, emphasis added)

> Many have in a great measure failed to receive the former rain. They have not obtained all the benefits that God has thus provided for them. They expect that the lack will be supplied by the latter rain. When the

richest abundance of grace shall be bestowed, they intend to open their hearts to receive it. They are making a terrible mistake. The work that God has begun in the human heart in giving his light and knowledge, must be continually going forward. Every individual must realize his own necessity. The heart must be emptied of every defilement, and cleansed for the indwelling of the Spirit. *It was by the confession and forsaking of sin, by earnest prayer and consecration of themselves to God, that the early disciples prepared for the outpouring of the Holy Spirit on the day of Pentecost. The same work, only in greater degree, must be done now. Then the human agent had only to ask for the blessing, and wait for the Lord to perfect the work concerning him.* It is God who began the work, and he will finish his work, making man complete in Jesus Christ. But there must be no neglect of the grace represented by the former rain. Only those who are living up to the light they have, will receive greater light. *Unless we are daily advancing in the exemplification of the active Christian virtues, we shall not recognize the manifestations of the Holy Spirit in the latter rain. It may be falling on hearts all around us, but we shall not discern or receive it.* (White, *The Review and Herald*, March 2, 1897, emphasis added)

The latter rain is to fall upon the people of God. A mighty angel is to come down from heaven, and the whole earth is to be lighted with his glory. Are we ready to take part in the glorious work of the third angel? Are our vessels ready to receive the heavenly dew? Have we defilement and sin in the heart? If so, let us cleanse the soul temple, and prepare for the showers of the latter rain. The refreshing from the presence of the Lord will never come to hearts filled with impurity. May God help us to die to self, that Christ, the hope of glory, may be formed within! I must have the Spirit of God in my heart. I can never go forward to do the great work of God, unless the Holy Spirit rests upon my soul. "As the hart panteth after the water brooks, so panteth my soul after thee, O God." The day of judgment is upon us. O that we may wash our robes of character, and make them white in the blood of the Lamb! (White, *The Review and Herald*, April 21, 1891)

Chapter 12

The Removal of the Testimonies

For readers who are not familiar with the history of Adventism, the three main founders of the church, which grew out of the second great awakening and the Millerite movement of 1844, were James and Ellen White and Joseph Bates. Between 1844 and her death in 1915, Ellen wrote a series of books called *Testimonies for the Church*, in which she related what God had shown her about issues facing individuals and the church as a whole. Sometimes, her testimonies were well received, but often, they were not.

On Sabbath, September 17, 2016, I came across the following statement by Ellen White, which was released for the first time by the White Estate in July 2015. Until that time, this prediction had never been publicly published and is nestled in among the 50,000 pages released by the estate, so it's hard to say how many Adventists are aware of it now. Her statement struck me with full force.

White was writing to G. I. Butler, who had recently resigned from the presidency of the governing body of the church, the General Conference, (he would resume that position in 1877) and was, at this time, in doubt of her prophetic gift. She informed him: "I am now of the opinion that the Testimonies will not live among God's people. They will be removed. I have some light on this point but cannot now give it. Said Christ, 'I have many things to say unto you but ye cannot bear them now'" (*Letters and Manuscripts*, vol. 2).

In her later writings, White made statements warning that the prophetic gift could someday be extinguished among Adventists, but none of her subsequent statements are so direct as to plainly say it *will* happen. This statement, of course, doesn't mean it is inevitable, but only that God, knowing the future, sees the choice the church will make.

Notice above that in 1875, White had "light on this point but cannot now give it." Did she give more light on it later? She did. We'll look at some of it momentarily, but first, you might ask, Doesn't Ellen White also say the church will not fall—that God's denominated people will remain faithful to the end? She does. How can both statements be true?

Many Adventist leaders and laymen unfortunately do not understand what White meant by "denominated people" or "the church." The Scripture, specifically the statements of Christ, and those of White agree that the church, God's denominated people, are those who maintain a vital connection with Him and whose names are written in the book of life.

Here are some statements from Scripture and Ellen White on this:

God has a church. It is not the great cathedral, neither is it the national establishment, neither is it the various denominations; it is the people who love God and keep His commandments. "Where two or three are gathered together in My name, there am I in the midst of them." *Where Christ is even among the humble few, this is Christ's church, for the presence of the high and holy One who inhabiteth eternity can alone constitute a church.* (White, *Manuscript Releases*, vol. 17, p. 81, emphasis added)

Fear not, little flock; for it is your Father's good pleasure to give you the kingdom. (Luke 12:32)

Even as Abraham believed God, and it was accounted to him for righteousness. Know ye therefore that they which are of faith, the same are the children of Abraham. (Galatians 3:6, 7)

"And there shall be no more curse; but the throne of God and of the Lamb shall be in it; and his servants shall serve him: and they shall see His face; and His name shall be in their foreheads." Revelation 22:3, 4.

Who are these?—God's denominated people—those who on this earth have witnessed to their loyalty. Who are they?—Those who have kept the commandments of God and the faith of Jesus; those who have owned the Crucified One as their Saviour. (White, *Our High Calling*, p. 345)

The church may appear as about to fall, but it does not fall. It remains, while the sinners in Zion will be sifted out—the chaff separated from the precious wheat. This is a terrible ordeal, but nevertheless it must take place. None but those who have been overcoming by the blood of the Lamb and the word of their testimony will be found with the loyal and true, without spot or stain of sin, without guile in their mouths. We must be divested of our self-righteousness and arrayed in the righteousness of Christ. (White, *Selected Messages*, book 2, p. 380)

What does the last statement mean? The church that appears as though it is about to fall but does not and goes through until the end are the faithful who, under intense persecution, appear to be on the verge of letting go of all hope and capitulating in despair. It is these who finally press through the darkness by faith and overcome by the blood of the Lamb and the word of their testimony because they love not their lives unto death (see Rev. 12:11–17).

Nominal Adventists and nominal Christians who have never been converted are in for a hard time. Some of them may, at the eleventh hour, consent to have their blinders removed and join those who make a covenant with God by sacrifice.

Those who press through the darkness described in inspiration are anything but anarchists. By overcoming the threatening of persecution, they heed the call to come into line under the generalship of Christ. Their victory renders them fearless, and there will be perfect organization among them (see White, *Early Writings*, p. 279).

Many of our current pastors and leaders seem to think this order will be the structure of the General Conference. That there will be perfect order and discipline in the ranks of the remnant is clear, but in the same way the Jewish leaders of Christ's day rejected the call of God and violently opposed His messenger, John the Baptist, we've been told the Seventh-day Adventist Church will also reject the *Testimonies*—"they will no longer live among God's people. *They will be removed.*"

How will they be removed? Consider the following dream given in March of 1867, while James and Ellen White were on their way home to Battle Creek, Michigan, the headquarters of the church at that time:

> I dreamed that I was in Battle Creek looking out from the side glass at the door and saw a company marching up to the house, two and two. They looked stern and determined. I knew them well and turned to open the parlor door to receive them, but thought I would look again. The scene was changed. The company now presented the appearance of a Catholic procession. One bore in his hand a cross, another a reed. And

as they approached, the one carrying a reed made a circle around the house, saying three times: "This house is proscribed. The goods must be confiscated. They have spoken against our holy order." Terror seized me, and I ran through the house, out of the north door, and found myself in the midst of a company, some of whom I knew, but I dared not speak a word to them for fear of being betrayed. I tried to seek a retired spot where I might weep and pray without meeting eager, inquisitive eyes wherever I turned. I repeated frequently: "If I could only understand this! If they will tell me what I have said or what I have done!"

I wept and prayed much as I saw our goods confiscated. I tried to read sympathy or pity for me in the looks of those around me, and marked the countenances of several whom I thought would speak to me and comfort me if they did not fear that they would be observed by others. I made one attempt to escape from the crowd, but seeing that I was watched, I concealed my intentions. I commenced weeping aloud, and saying: "If they would only tell me what I have done or what I have said!" My husband, who was sleeping in a bed in the same room, heard me weeping aloud and awoke me. My pillow was wet with tears, and a sad depression of spirits was upon me. (White, *Testimonies for the Church*, vol. 1, pp. 577, 578)

Commenting on the dream in his biography series, Arthur White, grandson of James and Ellen, suggested the dream was given as a warning of the treatment his grandmother was about to receive from the leaders at Battle Creek on their return.[9] While that is a valid application, the dream contains a broader warning for all of us of what is ahead.

The following quotes give us more information on the rejection of the *Testimonies*. The first one below was written to the church leaders at Battle Creek, many of whom, like Elder Butler, were in doubt regarding the full inspiration of the *Testimonies*. As you read, notice not only the process of removal but also the hopeful outcome she describes as she concludes.

I have been shown that the spirit of the world is fast leavening the church. You are following the same path as did ancient Israel. There is the same falling away from your holy calling as God's peculiar people. You are having fellowship with the unfruitful works of darkness. Your concord with unbelievers has provoked the Lord's displeasure.

---

[9] See Arthur White, *Ellen White: The Progressive Years (1862–1876)*, Vol. 2 (Hagerstown, MD: Review and Herald Publishing Association, 1988), pp. 207, 208.

You know not the things that belong to your peace, and they are fast being hid from your eyes. Your neglect to follow the light will place you in a more unfavorable position than the Jews upon whom Christ pronounced a woe.

I have been shown that unbelief in the testimonies has been steadily increasing as the people backslide from God. It is all through our ranks, all over the field. But few know what our churches are to experience. I saw that at present we are under divine forbearance; but no one can say how long this will continue....

The patience of God has an object, but you are defeating it. He is allowing a state of things to come that you would fain see counteracted by and by, but it will be too late. God commanded Elijah to anoint the cruel and deceitful Hazael king over Syria, that he might be a scourge to idolatrous Israel. Who knows whether God will not give you up to the deceptions you love? Who knows but that the preachers who are faithful, firm, and true may be the last who shall offer the gospel of peace to our unthankful churches? It may be that the destroyers are already training under the hand of Satan and only wait the departure of a few more standard-bearers to take their places, and with the voice of the false prophet cry, Peace, peace, when the Lord hath not spoken peace. I seldom weep, but now I find my eyes blinded with tears; they are falling upon my paper as I write. It may be that ere long all prophesyings among us will be at an end, and the voice which has stirred the people may no longer disturb their carnal slumbers....

I know that many think far too favorably of the present time. These ease-loving souls will be engulfed in the general ruin. Yet we do not despair. We have been inclined to think that where there are no faithful ministers, there can be no true Christians; but this is not the case. God has promised that where the shepherds are not true he will take charge of the flock himself. God has never made the flock wholly dependent upon human instrumentalities. But the days of purification of the church are hastening on apace. God will have a people pure and true. In the mighty sifting soon to take place, we shall be better able to measure the strength of Israel. The signs reveal that the time is near when the Lord will manifest that his fan is in his hand, and he will thoroughly purge his floor....

The Lord has faithful servants, who in the shaking, testing time will be disclosed to view. There are precious ones now hidden who have not bowed the knee to Baal.... But it may be under a rough and uninviting exterior the pure brightness of a genuine Christian character will be revealed. In the day-time we look toward heaven, but do not see the stars. They are there, fixed in the firmament, but the eye cannot distinguish them. In the night we behold their genuine luster....

Then will the church of Christ appear "fair as the moon, clear as the sun, and terrible as an army with banners." ....

The church cannot measure herself by the world nor by the opinion of men nor by what she once was. Her faith and her position in the world as they now are must be compared with what they would have been if her course had been continually onward and upward. The church will be weighed in the balances of the sanctuary. If her moral character and spiritual state do not correspond with the benefits and blessings God has conferred upon her, she will be found wanting. (White, *Testimonies for the Church*, vol. 5, pp. 75, 77, 79, 80, 83)

Six years later, she warned again:

There will be a hatred kindled against the testimonies which is satanic. The workings of Satan will be to unsettle the faith of the churches in them, for this reason: Satan cannot have so clear a track to bring in his deceptions and bind up souls in his delusions if the warnings and reproofs and counsels of the Spirit of God are heeded. (White, *Selected Messages*, book 1, p. 48)

As Adventists, our mutual obligation to one another is to be good stewards of our findings of truth. This finding is like when the priests under Joash found the scroll of the law and realized Israel was under God's judgment and would be rejected and dispossessed as He had said through Moses unless they repented. What if the priests had been unfaithful and not shared the warning? Aren't we under obligation to share this?

Look at what Moses said to Israel in Deuteronomy 32 and how he riveted his warning in the national conscience by a song, warning that apostasy would indeed occur. This was as much his parting legacy as were the blessings he pronounced on the twelve tribes that same day. The record says his warning was fully accepted by Israel at that time, and they mourned the death of Moses for a full month. Similarly, shouldn't this inspired warning as well as this promise of a remnant be made as public as possible to all the citizens of spiritual Israel?

I would be so glad to be wrong about these things and go along with those in the church who claim Ellen White taught the triumph of the Seventh-day Adventist corporation. I'm persuaded, however, that those who

> *I would be so glad to be wrong about these things and go along with those in the church who claim Ellen White taught the triumph of the Seventh-day Adventist corporation. I'm persuaded, however, that those who teach such things are like the Jews who, denying the prophecies of Moses, said, "The temple of the Lord, the temple of the Lord." Thus, while it's clear that we are to remain connected to the church through membership wherever possible, we should not be surprised if we find ourselves on the outside for speaking against this holy order— our testimony silenced within Adventism despite our best efforts to maintain the bond of love and unity among us.*

teach such things are like the Jews who, denying the prophecies of Moses, said, "The temple of the Lord, the temple of the Lord." Thus, while it's clear that we are to remain connected to the church through membership wherever possible, we should not be surprised if we find ourselves on the outside for speaking against this holy order—our testimony silenced within Adventism despite our best efforts to maintain the bond of love and unity among us.

Again, here is a wonderful promise of the care of God over His church that was partly quoted above:

Where two or three are present who love and obey the commandments of God, Jesus there presides, let it be in the desolate place of the earth, in the wilderness, in the city, [or] enclosed in prison walls. The glory of God has penetrated the prison walls, flooding with glorious beams of heavenly light the darkest dungeon. His saints may suffer, but their sufferings will, like the apostles of old, spread their faith and win souls to Christ and glorify His holy name. The bitterest opposition expressed by those who hate God's great moral standard of righteousness should not and will not shake the steadfast soul who trusts fully in God.

All things shall work together for good to those who love God. "This is the love of God, that we keep His commandments." They that will be doers of the word are building securely, and the tempest and storm of persecution will not shake their foundation, because their souls are rooted to the eternal Rock. (White, *Manuscript Releases*, vol. 17, pp. 81, 82)

Silencing the Two Witnesses

The removal of the *Testimonies* in Adventism is similar to the silencing of the two witnesses by the beast from the bottomless pit in the streets of Sodom and Egypt. This removal and silencing in the church and the world has been progressing since apostolic times, but it is accelerating. It reached an important milestone when the US Congress invited the pope and acknowledged his moral leadership in 2015. It reached another milestone in 2017 when most Protestant denominations denied the validity of the Protestant Reformation on its 500th anniversary (Martin Luther's posting of his famous *Ninety-five Theses*, October 31, 1517). Since then, the two witnesses of Revelation 11 have especially come under direct attack in Western culture.

However, this is about to change. It is during the darkest night that the stars shine brightest. At midnight, the cry is heard: "Behold the bridegroom cometh, go ye out to meet Him" (Matt. 25:6). As we look at the signs, can we hear in them the Lord's gracious invitation to arise and shine? It's time to trim our lamps and respond from our hearts to the fathomless love of God.

> And they that be wise shall shine as the brightness of the firmament; and they that turn many to righteousness as the stars for ever and ever.... Many shall be purified, and made white, and tried; but the wicked shall do wickedly: and none of the wicked shall understand; but the wise shall understand. (Daniel 12:3, 10)

To recap, since 9/11, we have especially been in a sealing time, when the winds of strife have been held back, but that is about to change. When it does, the wicked will continue in their denial, but the righteous will recognize the start of the shaking—the change to the hour of judgment—by 1) a major earthquake, literal and/or political, 2) the latter rain, which is and will be poured out, and 3) by the *Testimonies* eventually being removed and the witnesses put to silence in the nominal church, which is also happening now. However, the two witnesses will be enshrined in the remnant by the new covenant seal of God, and 4) the final phase of this sealing will take place when the trumpets begin to sound.

Chapter 13

Nashville and Great Balls of Fire

Earlier, I reviewed how the events of 9/11 were a partial fulfillment of Ellen White's dream of explosions that destroyed the entire city block of the World Trade Center and suggested two lessons from it: 1) We are in the sealing time now, when the four winds of strife have been held back; and 2) when those winds are let go the scenes described there will be repeated on a larger scale.

One reason many Adventists don't see any fulfillment of White's vision in what occurred on September 11, 2001, is that it's not an exact fit. She said, "I heard explosion after explosion. I rose up quickly in bed, and saw from my window large balls of fire. Jetting out were sparks, in the form of arrows, and buildings were being consumed." While it's true that this account does not exactly match what occurred on 9/11, it should be remembered that the scene was repeated twice, indicating there will be two fulfillments.

In Matthew 24, Christ did something similar in combining two events: the destruction of Jerusalem and the end-time destruction of the world. Not all of His description was fulfilled in AD 70, when Jerusalem was destroyed, yet the destruction of Jerusalem fulfilled much of His prediction. And the rest will be fulfilled as well before His return. In the same way, the first fulfillment of White's vision on 9/11 met most of the elements; the final fulfillment will meet the rest, including the balls of fire.

In 1904, two years before her 9/11 dream, White had another related dream. In this one, the Lord showed her explicitly that one of the main judgments that will come on the cities for their wickedness will be balls of fire:

> When I was at Nashville [in the summer of 1904], I had been speaking to the people, and in the night season, there was an immense ball of fire that came right from heaven and settled in Nashville. There were flames going out like arrows from that ball; houses were being consumed; houses were tottering and falling. Some of our people were standing there. "It is just as we expected," they said, "we expected this." Others were wringing their hands in agony and crying unto God for mercy. "You knew it," said they, "you knew that this was coming, and never said a word to warn us!" They seemed as though they would almost tear them to pieces, to think they had never told them or given them any warning at all. (White, *Letters and Manuscripts*, vol. 20)

Notice in this dream that the ball of fire fell specifically in Nashville, "where they were casting buildings with pillars" (*Letters and Manuscripts*, vol. 19). In 1897, the Centennial Exposition was held in Nashville to celebrate the 100th anniversary of the city's founding. For that occasion, the city, which viewed itself as the Athens of the south, built an exact replica of the Greek Parthenon, complete with a forty-two-foot idol of Athena,

Figure 7: The Parthenon of Nashville, Tennessee

the goddess of Athens called "the protector of cities." Surrounding the Parthenon were multiple temporary buildings made from brick, wood, and plaster casts. Today, only the Parthenon remains and is the most prominent building with pillars in Nashville.

Curiously, the people of Nashville have something of an obsession with fireballs. According to one source, the most popular whiskey produced and consumed in Nashville is Fireball Whiskey, and the logo of their National Football League team, the Tennessee Titans, is a fireball.

Interestingly, the Ellen G. White Estate asserts that the dream has no direct connection to Nashville:

> Some point to an unpublished sermon delivered in 1905 in which Ellen White described a dream she received several months earlier of seeing a ball of fire coming from heaven that "settled in Nashville" (Ms 188, 1905). Notably, she related the same dream seven other times between 1904 and 1909, but described the fiery ball as coming "down upon the world" or "the earth." She made no mention of the city as a target in her report of the dream the very next day, or in later published sermons or writings. Taking into account all of her related statements, we do not believe she was singling out Nashville above any other city, but that she understood the scene to be representative of the widespread destruction the Bible predicts will occur prior to and at Christ's return, and the need for every person to be spiritually prepared for that grand event.[10]

Although White stated, "There was an immense ball of fire that came right from heaven and settled in Nashville," the estate believes this warning was not specifically about Nashville. This may explain why the Seventh-day Adventist Church has made no official effort to share these warnings in Nashville, in this way fulfilling the prophecy concerning those who were angry because people knew these things were coming but remained silent.

To be fair, the estate is correct to point out that Nashville is not the only city singled out by White. In other places, she did indeed say destruction will come upon all the cities one after another: "The wrath of God is preparing to come upon all the cities—not all at once but one after another. And if the terrible punishment in one city does not cause

---

[10] "Statements Mistakenly Attributed to Ellen G. White," Ellen G. White Estate, https://whiteestate.org/legacy/issues-faq-mist-html/#mistaken-section-b3 (accessed Oct. 15, 2023).

the inhabitants of other cities to be afraid and seek repentance, their time will come" (*Letters and Manuscripts*, vol. 17).

Nevertheless, there is good reason, based on the dream, to conclude that Nashville will be among the first of the cities to receive these judgments. How do we know that? Because when these judgments fall upon Nashville, it is a surprise. It is a surprise to the Seventh-day Adventists who knew this was going to happen because they said, "We knew that the judgments of God were coming upon the earth, but we did not know they would come so soon." It's also an overwhelming surprise to the general public because they exclaim, "You knew! Why then did you not tell us? We did not know" (*Letters and Manuscripts*, vol. 19).

Since both groups are surprised and because these judgments will "come upon all the cities—not all at once but one after another," we can conclude Nashville is among the first.

However, the larger question is whether this event in White's dream is also found in Scripture. Consider the first three trumpets:

> The first angel sounded, and there followed hail and fire mingled with blood, and they were cast upon the earth: and the third part of trees was burnt up, and all green grass was burnt up. And the second angel sounded, and as it were a great mountain burning with fire was cast into the sea: and the third part of the sea became blood; And the third part of the creatures which were in the sea, and had life, died; and the third part of the ships were destroyed. And the third angel sounded, and there fell a great star from heaven, burning as it were a lamp, and it fell upon the third part of the rivers, and upon the fountains of waters; And the name of the star is called Wormwood: and the third part of the waters became wormwood; and many men died of the waters, because they were made bitter. (Revelation 8:7–11)

Notice when the first trumpet sounds, "hail and fire mingled with blood" are "cast upon the earth" and burn up all the grass and a third of the trees. This text implies that the hail is no ordinary hail because it is combined with fire that consumes a large part of the earth's vegetation, suggesting that the "hail" itself is actually brimstone—ignited sulfurous balls of fire. That this hail and fire are mingled with blood implies that, unlike normal hail, this hail is not only deadly to plants but also consumes animals and human life.

This agrees with the account of the destruction of Sodom and Gomorrah: "Then the LORD rained upon Sodom and upon Gomorrah brimstone [a hail of burning sulfurous rock] and fire from the LORD out of heaven" (Gen. 19:24). In the case of Sodom and Gomorrah, not only were the cities destroyed, but the surrounding plain was turned from a fertile vale to a scorched, desolate wilderness that today borders the Dead Sea and is by far the lowest elevation on earth: 1,356 feet below sea level. Compare this with the two locations in North America that are below sea level: Death Valley and the Salton Sea, both less than 100 feet.

This judgment of the first trumpet is the precursor of the greater judgments of the second and third trumpets: "a great mountain burning with fire" is cast into the sea, and the third part of the sea became blood; and finally, a "great star from heaven" falls, "burning as it were a lamp upon the third part of the rivers, and upon the fountains of waters." This trumpet is also a leading candidate for the destruction of many cities because it is extensive, affecting a third of the rivers. Any object that causes this level of harm to fresh water sources may also cause the destruction of the surrounding cities.

In the fifth trumpet, the angel with the key to the bottomless pit opens it; the earth is darkened with its smoke, and locusts are given power to torture humanity for five months. Notice, however, that this plague only afflicts those who do not have the seal of God. We can conclude from this that by the time of the fifth trumpet, most, if not all, of the sealing work of the 144,000 is complete (see Rev. 7).

> Since 9/11, we have especially been in a sealing time, when the winds of strife have been held back, but that is about to change, and the judgment is about to become more evident in Adventism, Christianity at large, and the world.

To recap: Since 9/11, we have especially been in a sealing time, when the winds of strife have been held back, but that is about to change, and the judgment is about to become more evident in Adventism, Christianity at large, and the world.

Chapter 14

Mystery Babylon Rides Again

And there came one of the seven angels which had the seven vials, and talked with me, saying unto me, Come hither; I will shew unto thee the judgment of the great whore that sitteth upon many waters ... So he carried me away in the spirit into the wilderness: and I saw a woman sit upon a scarlet colored beast, full of names of blasphemy, having seven heads and ten horns.... And the angel said unto me, Wherefore didst thou marvel? I will tell thee the mystery of the woman, and of the beast that carrieth her, which hath the seven heads and ten horns. The beast that thou sawest was, and is not; and shall ascend out of the bottomless pit, and go into perdition: and they that dwell on the earth shall wonder, whose names were not written in the book of life from the foundation of the world, when they behold the beast that was, and is not, and yet is.... And he saith unto me, The waters which thou sawest, where the whore sitteth, are peoples, and multitudes, and nations, and tongues.... And the woman which thou sawest is that great city, which reigneth over the kings of the earth.

Revelation 17:1, 3, 7, 8, 15, 18.

The Coming Woke Theocracy

A couple years ago, an online article opened with a somewhat cynical but keen observation:

> Over a two day period in late March of 1979, the people of Iran held a groundbreaking referendum to turn their country into a theocratic Islamic Republic where the religious leaders ruled supreme.

According to the ... officials who counted the votes, 99.3% of the ballots were cast in favor of becoming an Islamic Republic.

(This bears a striking resemblance to Kim Jong Un winning a 2014 'election' in North Korea with 100% of the vote, or when Saddam Hussein won re-election in Iraq back in 2002 with 11.4 million votes in favor, and 0 against.)

Within months, a new constitution was drafted, and Iran became a theocracy.

In a theocracy, the rules and rituals of the official state religion become pervasive in everything– politics, education, business, news, entertainment, and even your daily routine– regardless of whether or not you're a believer... if you're even allowed to be a non-believer.

In its own way, the United States (and much of the West) is rapidly becoming a theocracy where the woke leftist religion similarly pervades our daily lives. (Simon Black, "The coming 'woke' American Theocracy," Sovereign Man, January 6, 2021)

Black goes on to make his case. He points to the tell-tale signs that a quasi-religious ideology is overtaking America. Rather than reciting his list here, which is long, somewhat depressing, and, for the most part, common knowledge, the question for all of us is whether this moral disintegration of Western and global culture is mentioned in Scripture.

The answer, of course, is yes. As it was in the woke days of Noah, Christ said, "so shall also the coming of the Son of man be" (Matt. 24:37). The beast of prophecy is currently on display in America and around the Western world in the persecution of those business owners who can't buy or sell unless they, in violation of their consciences, cater to the LGBT sector. Those who plead for biblical morality, affirm that "all lives matter" or gender is biologically based risk job loss, economic and social sanctions, and, in some locations, civil and criminal penalties for so-called hate crimes.

God's two witnesses are being silenced by the "beast that rises from the bottomless pit [who] will make war on them and conquer them and kill them, and their dead bodies will lie in the street of the great city that symbolically is called Sodom and Egypt, where their Lord was crucified" (Rev. 11:7, 8, ESV).

Notice where the witnesses are slain: in the streets of spiritual Sodom and Egypt. And notice by whom: the beast from the bottomless pit. This is the same beast from the same pit that the harlot, Mystery Babylon, rides: "The beast that thou sawest was, and is not; and shall ascend out of the bottomless pit, and go into perdition: and they that dwell on the earth shall wonder, whose names were not written in the book of life from the foundation of the world, when they behold the beast that was, and is not, and yet is" (17:8).

The beast of Revelation 11 and 17 is the same one that is wounded in chapter 13, but its wound is healed. The overarching feature of this beast's ideology is unthinking conformity to debasing humanistic laws and fables: All the world blindly wonders after it, idolizing and worshiping its false norms that displace an intelligent faith in the Word.

One of the most troubling recent examples of blind trust placed in human wisdom is the disproportionate COVID response that caused social pain and disruption far worse than did the pandemic itself. The unnecessary lockdowns caused an epidemic of adolescent and teen suicide; millions were made jobless, and thousands homeless, who had never been in that situation before. However, the majority of our well-fed leaders continued on their course.

The silver lining in this is that many of the persecuted became more open than ever before to the gospel of Christ. The harvest continues to ripen. The pressing question for all of us now is, How do we cooperate with the first angel to spread the everlasting gospel *effectively*?

Chapter 15

Cooperating with Christ

Given that a messenger is only as credible as his or her character, and given that it takes time to develop character, how do we proceed? There's an apparent tension between delivering an urgent message and the fact that character takes a lifetime to develop. Or is there? In my view, a balanced answer is given in the books *Education* and *The Ministry of Healing* by Ellen White. The whole church, new members and veterans, will all grow in grace and be prepared to meet Christ by following the inspired counsels on both how to live *and* bring in the harvest.

> "
> Given that a messenger is only as credible as his or her character, and given that it takes time to develop character, how do we proceed? There's an apparent tension between delivering an urgent message and the fact that character takes a lifetime to develop. Or is there?
> "

In just a few short chapters, these books tell us how to minister effectively. In chapters 9–14 of *The Ministry of Healing*, especially chapters 12 and 13, "Help for the Unemployed and the Homeless" and "The Helpless Poor," along with *Education*'s chapter 2, "The Eden School," White gave us the divine answer in any situation. In short order, she sets out our strategic evangelistic blueprint as well as that for our own character development.

This plan is foolproof in that if it's followed, it simultaneously accomplishes all three goals: 1) brings relief to the poor and the destitute; 2) effectively spreads the gospel and brings in the harvest; and 3) develops the character of the laborers *themselves*. I'd go so far as to say one reason Adventism has wandered in the wilderness for all these years is our unbelief in failing to follow these methods of labor, which are exactly what Christ would be doing if He was here in person.

Our failure to implement this program not only means we have not been the salt of the earth as we should be; it means as a church, we are blighted in the formation of our characters. As we know, or should know, this is the greatest failure in Adventism that has delayed the return of Christ. However vital the doctrines of the Sabbath, the sanctuary, and righteousness by faith may be, there is no substitute in character development for practical godliness and obedience to all the counsels of God. To be sealed in the truth, we have to both believe it and live it.

Personally, I'm renewing my commitment to these counsels, not only as my own plan for evangelism but also as my plea and call to Adventism to get with God's program. I would encourage all ministries, denominational and independent, to reevaluate their programs in the light of these chapters and consider whether God isn't calling us to come into line with His ideal of ministry: making agriculture and practical industries key components of our health and evangelistic outreach. As we do this, at the same time, we'll be meeting the needs of our brothers and sisters, many of whom are in unprecedented distress.

Regarding the specifics of what this program could look like, the goals are twofold: 1) meeting the basic needs of people while simultaneously 2) developing and training youth and adults as entrepreneur/agricultural/medical evangelists. To achieve both, I suggest building micro-manufacturing educational training centers with agriculture and health evangelism at the core of the program. As a means of skill training, mentoring, and covering tuition, student teams would build their own homes and hone their industrial skills by manufacturing products.

Reaching the Rich

The principles of evangelism for rich and poor are the same, but reaching the rich requires meeting different needs. Health evangelism in the form of cooking schools, restaurants, natural health sanitariums, etc. all have a role. Above, I suggested a program of micro-industry, agriculture, and health training centers. Modified for the rich, this model could be equally successful.

One of the shortcomings of most if not all self-supporting Adventist health and lifestyle centers is they expose their guests to short programs of less than a month. Many guests recover from chronic, lifestyle-induced diseases but, within a year, relapse into their old lifestyles, and their chronic conditions return. Why? Because they were cured physically but not spiritually. A significantly longer exposure and mentoring is needed so people are grounded spiritually and themselves equipped and motivated to be effective medical missionaries (For more on this, see *The Ministry of Healing*, chapter 14, "Ministry to the Rich").

As Americans and Adventists, we view ourselves as ready to rise to a challenge. Here is a divine challenge coupled with one of the greatest socioeconomic crises in American history. The motivation couldn't be greater: effective philanthropy, the salvation of other souls, and our own redemption. Those who accept the challenge and come into line with Christ and His methods will have no regrets. Like Christ, they will eventually see the travail of their souls and be satisfied.

To recap, since 9/11, we have especially been in a sealing time. The plan of evangelism given in the books *Education* and *The Ministry of Healing* is central to the sealing process. It not only effectively spreads the gospel and brings in the harvest; it also develops the character of the laborers themselves.

Chapter 16

The Abomination of Desolation

When ye therefore shall see the abomination of desolation, spoken of by Daniel the prophet, stand in the holy place, (whoso readeth, let him understand:) Then let them which be in Judaea flee into the mountains: Let him which is on the housetop not come down to take any thing out of his house ... But pray ye that your flight be not in the winter, neither on the sabbath day: For then shall be great tribulation, such as was not since the beginning of the world to this time, no, nor ever shall be. And except those days should be shortened, there should no flesh be saved: but for the elect's sake those days shall be shortened.

Matthew 24:15–17, 20–22

The prophecy of Christ regarding the abomination of desolation is singular in Scripture. It is the only instance where Christ points to a specific end-time prophecy and tells the church to both read and understand it. God is saying to the church, "This is important." Fortunately for us who live two millennia later, we have two historic fulfillments that can guide us in interpreting its final, most important application.

This prophecy was first fulfilled when the armies of Rome destroyed Jerusalem and the temple in AD 70. Shortly before this occurred, the Roman armies besieged Jerusalem, briefly occupying the holy area surrounding the city, but withdrew for a time before resuming their siege. The early Christians recognized the initial siege as a fulfillment of Christ's warning and Daniel's prophecy. The believers heeded the warning and, before the Roman armies returned, fled Jerusalem, and not one Christian perished in the final siege.

The prophecy was fulfilled again in AD 538, when papal Rome was given civil authority as the "corrector of heretics," and the true church was forced to flee again, this time into the wilderness for 1,260 years. At the end of this period, 1798, the political power of the pope was broken temporarily when Napoleon's general deposed him and took him captive.

The words of Christ and other passages of Scripture indicate, however, that the complete fulfillment of this prophecy is still in the future. The same pattern will exist: The mortal wound the beast received in 1798 will be healed, and the antichrist power will act quickly, with the speed of a leopard, to consolidate its power and eventually silence all opposition and suspend freedom and religious liberty. And with the strength of a bear and the iron grasp of a dragon, it will, at the end, compel the consciences of its subjects to submit to a false worship and counterfeit religion on pain of death.

> And I stood upon the sand of the sea, and saw a beast rise up out of the sea, having seven heads and ten horns, and upon his horns ten crowns, and upon his heads the name of blasphemy. And the beast which I saw was like unto a leopard, and his feet were as the feet of a bear, and his mouth as the mouth of a lion: and the dragon gave him his power, and his seat, and great authority. And I saw one of his heads as it were wounded to death; and his deadly wound was healed: and all the world wondered after the beast. And they worshipped the dragon which gave power unto the beast: and they worshipped the beast, saying, Who is like unto the beast? who is able to make war with him? And there was given unto him a mouth speaking great things and blasphemies; and power was given unto him to continue forty and two months. And he opened his mouth in blasphemy against God, to blaspheme his name, and his tabernacle, and them that dwell in heaven. And it was given unto him to make war with the saints, and to overcome them: and power was given him over all kindreds, and tongues, and nations. And all that dwell upon the earth shall worship him, whose names are not written in the book of life of the Lamb slain from the foundation of the world. (Revelation 13:1–8)

The two beasts of Revelation 13 who create this abomination of idolatry are, I assert, the final powers represented in Daniel 7 by the fourth beast. As we've seen above, the spirit of antichrist is already rampant throughout Western Christendom. Popular woke culture has rejected Christ; it is at war with Him, but soon, a specific series of events will catapult the revived beast with great teeth of iron and claws of brass (ref. Dan. 7:19; Rev. 13:2) back onto the world stage: As noted above, an earthquake of biblical proportions and/or perhaps war will arrest the course of human history and cause the healing of the mortally wounded beast. Let's now examine the prophecies describing the judgment of the beast and Babylon.

The Judgment of Babylon the Great

> And there came one of the seven angels which had the seven vials, and talked with me, saying unto me, Come hither; I will shew unto thee the judgment of the great whore that sitteth upon many waters. (Revelation 17:1)

The final atonement of Christ, the judgment of the living, and the judgment of Babylon are closely linked. They are all aspects of the final phase of the new covenant ministry of Christ, which, according to the ancient types, takes place in the Most Holy Place of the heavenly sanctuary. During this time, the church on earth is called out of Babylon by Christ; she is cleansed and clothed in her white wedding garment while Babylon the harlot is judged and finally destroyed.

In Revelation, this harlot is identified as "Mystery, Babylon the Great" (verse 5). Mystery Babylon is one of the most important topics covered in this book because the description of the fornicating woman in Revelation 17 is the clearest unmasking of her identity found in Scripture. However, this is not a simple or easy matter. Spiritual Babylon, according to Scripture, is a mystery beyond fallen human understanding. Her mysterious character is such a prominent feature of her identity that it is actually part of her name: "And upon her forehead was a name written, MYSTERY, BABYLON THE GREAT, THE MOTHER OF HARLOTS AND ABOMINATIONS OF THE EARTH."

"Babylon" is all capitalized in the King James Version because it is both her title and name. A few verses later, her mysterious nature and the cryptic nature of the beast she rides is underscored again. The angel who explains the mystery begins by saying, "And here is the mind which hath wisdom" (verse 9), indicating that understanding her identity requires more than human logic and reasoning; it requires divine revelation.

This is also underscored in the description of the beast she rides, which later morphs into her enemy: "Here is wisdom. Let him that hath understanding count the number of the beast: for it is the number of a man; and his number is Six hundred threescore and six" (13:18).

In order to understand the mystery of Babylon, we need to study the beast she rides; and if we want to understand the beast, we need to study her. The two go together—she rides the beast, and the beast carries her.

Chapter 17

Who and What Is Babylon?

Protestants, from the start of the Reformation until the last century, were unitedly agreed that spiritual Babylon was a symbol of the papacy. Recently, though, many Christians have become convinced that America has become the Babylon of prophecy. Who is right, the Protestant reformers or modern Christians? Both views contain elements of truth. I believe Babylon's power is manifested by the papacy *and* America, which are both depicted in Revelation 13 and 17.

On September 24, 2015, the papal phase was fulfilled in part when the pope addressed the American Congress. This was a significant fulfillment of this vision:

> And I stood upon the sand of the sea, and saw a beast rise up out of the sea, having seven heads and ten horns, and upon his horns ten crowns, and upon his heads the name of blasphemy. And the beast which I saw was like unto a leopard, and his feet were as the feet of a bear, and his mouth as the mouth of a lion: and the dragon gave him his power, and his seat, and great authority. And I saw one of his heads as it were wounded to death; and his deadly wound was healed: and all the world wondered after the beast. And they worshipped the dragon which gave power unto the beast: and they worshipped the beast, saying, Who is like unto the beast? who is able to make war with him? (Revelation 13:1–4)

Since 1798, when the pope was dethroned and taken captive by Napoleon, there have been a number of events contributing to the healing of the mortal wound of the beast. See Appendix D regarding the 1929 signing of the Lateran Treaty and the history behind the Lateran Palace.

Those events were milestones as well, but 2015 was notable because for the first time, the USA, a Protestant nation and leader of the free world, officially gave homage *as a nation* to the pope.

Yes, President Ronald Reagan sent the first US ambassador to Rome in 1984, but that was only his personal initiative. In 2015, all three branches of the American government bowed to the pope. The leading nation of the free world wondered after the beast.

What's Next?

Revelation 17 tells us in more detail what is about to follow. In verse 1, John is told he's about to be shown the judgment of the harlot, Babylon, by one of the angels who poured out the final plagues on her. This angel is likely the seventh, the one who completes the destruction of Babylon. This is a timing indicator to show us the judgment of Babylon is concurrent with and caused by all the plagues, especially the sixth and seventh (For more on this, see Revelation 16, especially the verses with references to Babylon, the beast, and his mark.)

Revelation 18 confirms that Babylon will be destroyed by certain plagues in one hour. The text also indicates that one of the means God employs to humble and dethrone Babylon is her enemies. And it reveals that Babylon at this point controls the global economy.

> And I heard another voice from heaven, saying, Come out of her, my people, that ye be not partakers of her sins, and that ye receive not of her plagues. For her sins have reached unto heaven, and God hath remembered her iniquities.... And the kings of the earth, who have committed fornication and lived deliciously with her, shall bewail her, and lament for her, when they shall see the smoke of her burning, *Standing afar off for the fear of her torment, saying, Alas, alas, that great city Babylon, that mighty city! for in one hour is thy judgment come. And the merchants of the earth shall weep and mourn over her; for no man buyeth their merchandise any more* ... The merchants of these things, which were made rich by her, shall stand afar off for the fear of her torment, weeping and wailing, And saying, Alas, alas, that great city, that was clothed in fine linen, and purple, and scarlet, and decked with gold, and precious stones, and pearls! For in one hour so great riches is come to nought [see the rest of the chapter for more details confirming the economic nature of the final phase of Babylon]. (Revelation 18:4, 5, 9–11, 15–17, emphasis added).

If Babylon at that point was merely the papacy, the rulers and merchants of the earth would not mourn her demise and be in extreme distress. That the final phase of Babylon is Protestant America ruling the world and controlling the global economy through the political power of the beast is shown by the fact that in Scripture, she is depicted as the producer and controller of the world's wealth. This is in contrast to the papacy, which, although fabulously wealthy, has always been a consumer of the world's wealth, not a producer.

Seven Mountains

When John is shown Babylon's judgment in Revelation 17, what does he see? He's shown a woman in a wilderness on a scarlet beast that has seven heads and ten horns, with ten crowns on its horns. As suggested a moment ago, at the start of this narrative, the woman, Babylon, is the papacy, gorgeously arrayed in purple and scarlet, decked with gold, jewels, and pearls and holding a golden cup in her hand full of her abominations and fornications.

A notable sign that the woman is under divine judgment during this time is she and the beast she rides are in a desolate wilderness. In the Hebrew service, on the Day of Atonement, the scapegoat, a symbol of Satan, was led into the wilderness to its death by a fit man (see Lev. 16). By the end of Revelation 17, Babylon is in her final phase of judgment.

The angel explains to John that the heads of the scarlet beast have a dual application: They are both seven mountains and seven kings or kingdoms. "And here is the mind which hath wisdom. The seven heads are seven mountains, on which the woman sitteth. And there are seven kings: five are fallen, and one is, and the other is not yet come; and when he cometh, he must continue a short space" (verses 9, 10).

Mountains and high places in Scripture have always been associated with religious worship among the heathen and Jews. The tribes go "up" to Mount Zion to worship at their appointed feasts; the false gods are found on mounts such as Olympus and Hermon. The law was given from Mount Sinai. Revival occurred on Mount Carmel. Christ was transfigured on the mount. He ascended from the Mount of Olives, and at the close of the millennium, He will return and descend with the New Jerusalem on the Mount of Olives. And Satan aspires to rule God's people, symbolized by Mount Zion, which is the mountain on the north side of Jerusalem (see Ps. 48:2). "For thou hast said in thine heart, I will ascend into heaven, I will exalt my throne above the stars of God: I will sit also upon the mount of the congregation, in the sides of the north" (Isa. 14:13).

As mentioned earlier, in Scripture, a woman is used to represent a church: a pure woman, a faithful church; and an impure woman, an apostate church. Babylon is labeled "the mother of harlots," which tells us she has impure daughters, apostate churches originating from her, the mother. However, notice in Revelation 13 that when she was wounded, it was a wound to only one of the seven heads. Which head was wounded in 1798? Catholicism. The heads of her daughters were unscathed. Although European Protestant churches had replaced Catholicism as the state religion of their respective nations, these were left intact when Napoleon humbled the papacy.

The seven heads of the beast, described as seven mountains, are, in a secondary sense, the seven hills of Rome, but in a primary sense, the harlot and her harlot daughters, the main branches of Western Christianity: Catholicism, Swiss, Dutch, and Scottish Calvinism, Lutheranism, Anglicanism/Episcopalianism, Evangelical Fundamentalism—Baptist/Pentecostalism/other—and fringe churches such as Jehovah's Witnesses, Mormons, Christian Scientists, etc. When the woman rides again as the sixth head, six of her daughters, the Protestant churches, have returned to her fold, for a total of seven.

Seven Kings

Revelation 17:18 also tells us Mystery Babylon is that great city that reigns over the *kings* of the earth. The seven heads of the beast she rides are also the seven kings or nations by whom she rules.

Many good Bible expositors have suggested the seven heads of the beast are a *succession* of governments, kingdoms, or popes. I suggest the first six heads are *concurrent*, like the heads of the four-headed leopard of Daniel 7, rather than a succession because it is these powers/heads that support the woman. Initially, I would expect five European powers will form an alliance with her (she is the sixth), and not long afterward, one more will briefly join them, for a total of seven, before she is overthrown.

The return of European Protestants to the fold of Rome is well advanced. In the late 1990s, the Lutherans of Germany reunited with Rome by forming an ecumenical alliance, and in the following years, the Anglicans, some branches of Orthodoxy, and many of America's Evangelicals have followed suit by doing the same. The last part of the prophecy that remains unfulfilled is the combining of the seven fallen churches, with the seven kings, the state. However, according to the prophecy, this part, when it comes, it will be with the speed of a leopard (see Rev. 13:2).

Now notice the following sequence outlined in Revelation 13: *Before* the lamb-like beast bids the earth to make an image of the first beast, the wound of the first beast, the papacy, is healed, and all the world wonders after it. This is the revival of the Holy Roman Empire in Europe. It will not use that name, but it will be its reincarnation. Ellen White indicated that while Romanism will be reinstated in Europe, America will chart its own course; and rather than adopting the papacy here, it will make an image of it: "Romanism in the Old World and apostate Protestantism in the New will pursue a similar course toward those who honor all the divine precepts" (*The Great Controversy*, p. 615).

> The return of European Protestants to the fold of Rome is well advanced. In the late 1990s, the Lutherans of Germany reunited with Rome by forming an ecumenical alliance, and in the following years, the Anglicans, some branches of Orthodoxy, and many of America's Evangelicals have followed suit by doing the same.

All of Revelation 17 describes Babylon's weighing process by Christ in the balances of the heavenly sanctuary. The harlot, Babylon, and the beast she rides are both scarlet, a symbol of their guilt and murder of the innocent. And they are full of the names of blasphemy as they impose a counterfeit worship and religion of human idolatry.

In Revelation 14, the second angel announces the fall of Babylon, followed immediately by a third angel who warns that anyone who takes the mark of the beast, a reference to 666, will drink of the undiluted wrath of God—the strongest warning found in Scripture.

Chapter 18

The Eighth Head and Ten Horns

In the last chapter, we examined the seven heads of the beast of Revelation 13 and 17, which were both mountains and kings and showed their connection to the fallen churches of Christendom, the man of sin, and the nations of Europe. Now we come to the eighth head. Notice in the prophecy that the eighth is in a separate category from the first seven. The eighth is not depicted as a head that supports the woman but instead, along with the ten horns, overthrows her, strips her naked, eats her flesh, and burns her with fire (see Rev. 17:16). It is these ten horns of American apostate Protestantism, together with the civil power of the Lamb-like beast, that dethrone her while at the same time creating an image of her. It is this beast of the eighth head, the antichrist, that wages the final war on the Lamb and is defeated by Him.

> And the ten horns which thou sawest are ten kings, which have received no kingdom as yet; but receive power as kings one hour with the beast. These have one mind, and shall give their power and strength unto the beast. These shall make war with the Lamb, and the Lamb shall overcome them: for he is Lord of lords, and King of kings: and they that are with him are called, and chosen, and faithful.... And the ten horns which thou sawest upon the beast, these shall hate the whore, and shall make her desolate and naked, and shall eat her flesh, and burn her with fire. For God hath put in their hearts to fulfil his will, and to agree, and give their kingdom unto the beast, until the words of God shall be fulfilled. (Revelation 17:12–14, 16, 17)

Ellen White confirmed that these ten horns are apostate Protestantism. "What is it that gives its kingdom to this power [referring to the eighth head]? Protestantism, a power which, while professing to have the temper and spirit of a lamb and to be allied to Heaven, speaks with the voice of a dragon. It is moved by a power from beneath" (*Maranatha*, p. 187).

The Battle of Armageddon reaches its climax here as Protestantism, under the leadership of the man of sin, the final antichrist, and spiritualism combine to make war on the Lamb (see Rev. 17:14; 16:12–16).

To summarize, the scarlet beast that carries the woman has seven heads, which are both mountains and kings/kingdoms. We know from prophecy and past history that Babylon is a corrupt alliance of church and state. When the mortally wounded head, the sixth, is healed, we can expect it will appear suddenly in Europe with the reincarnation of the Holy Roman Empire. This power will be challenged and toppled in America by apostate Protestantism, which will pay homage to the image of the beast, the son of perdition, the antichrist.[iv]

Chapter 19

The 666 Mystery

Here is wisdom. Let him that hath understanding count the number of the beast: for it is the number of a man; and his number is Six hundred threescore and six.

Revelation 13:18

One of the most gripping stories of the Old Testament is the downfall of ancient Babylon. Those who aren't familiar with it may want to read the account, which tells how, on the night of King Belshazzar's demise, the first word of doom written on the wall by the bloodless hand was *mene*. Inspiration interprets *mene* as "God hath numbered thy kingdom and finished it" (Dan. 5:26).

As ancient Babylon was divinely judged in the courts of heaven when the limit of its wickedness was full, in the same way, the beast and Mystery Babylon have been assigned a divine limit beyond which they cannot go. When the divine limit is reached, then, like ancient Babylon, they will be "weighed in the balance and found wanting."

The intercession of Christ for the harlot will end. The number 666, the "number of a man," is connected to that divine limit.

White and Miller on 666

There is only one reference to the number 666 in the writings of Ellen White, and the number is believed to have been inserted by the editor of the tract, Joseph Bates:

> I saw all that "would not receive the mark of the Beast, and of his Image, in their foreheads or in their hands," could not buy or sell.

[Revelation 13:15–17.] *I saw that the number (666) of the Image Beast was made up;* [Revelation 13:18.] and that it was the Beast that changed the Sabbath, and the Image Beast had followed on after, and kept the Pope's, and not God's Sabbath. And all we were required to do, was to give up God's Sabbath, and keep the Pope's, and then we should have the mark of the Beast, and of his image. (White, *A Word to the Little Flock*, p. 19, emphasis added)

What did Ellen White mean by the number being "made up"? The context suggests 666 stands for the "made up" tradition of Sunday sacredness. However, it has become clear that it includes more than that. Any human laws that do not harmonize with the law of God are "made up" by mankind. The mark of the beast, which bears the number 666, includes all blasphemous reverence or worship of human laws or tradition that supplants a clear command of God. As the West rejects Judeo-Christian values, its culture is being transformed into the culture of antichrist.

William Miller, in Lecture V(5) of his series of lectures in 1843,[11] presented his case that 666 is the number of years pagan Rome lasted from the time it first entered a league of treaty with the Jews in 158 BC until the fall of Roman paganism in AD 508.[12]

Miller's arguments are generally rejected today, but in my opinion, most points are scriptural. The number 666 could, as Miller held, point to the divine number of days allotted to the beast in the same way the days of ancient Babylon were numbered and ended by the word of the Lord, *mene*, but with this difference: At the end, they may point to a literal 666-day rule of the antichrist (For more on the numerical properties of 666, contrasting it with 153, another scriptural number, see Appendix E).

However, parts of the same prophecy indicate that 666 includes more than this. One of the weaknesses of Miller's application of 666 to only the duration of the antichrist is that it doesn't account for two of the key identifiers: 1) the mark is placed on the forehead or hand; and 2) the mark exposes and identifies those loyal to the beast.

Many Christians now think the mark is some kind of electronic tracking device augmented with artificial intelligence (AI) that will be implanted in the hand or forehead and directly linked to the brain. At the moment, that kind of technology is repulsive to most people, but the

---

[11] See William Miller, *Evidence from Scripture and History of the Second Coming of Christ About the Year 1843*. Boston: Joshua V. Himes Publisher, 1842.

[12] The 666 years suggested by Miller are subject to the same error as is the initial 1843 date due to Miller's failure to account for the lack of a 0 year between the BC and AD eras.

numbers are growing who see it as a quantum leap forward. Imagine if you could do your math like a supercomputer. On the other hand, imagine if someone hacks your brain.

Most technologies are neutral. They can be used for a good purpose, like tracking the migration of birds, or an evil purpose, like eavesdropping on your every word and movement and possibly even tracking your thoughts and inflicting punishment if "Big Brother" finds them objectionable.

Today, with ubiquitous surveillance technology and advancements in electronic implants, it is not hard to envision a high-tech solution used to enforce compliance to all the dictates of the antichrist system.

As the lamb-like beast asserts its claim to unquestioning obedience, like Nebuchadnezzar, it will construct and erect an image of the first beast, claiming its will should be upheld with the rigor of a modern Inquisition.

The same series of events that catapults the first beast of Revelation 13 back onto the world stage (possibly a combination of megaquakes and wars) sets the stage for the advent of the second, lamb-like beast. This second beast may work closely, at first, with the papacy to restore order and world peace, but its goal from the beginning will be its own global aggrandizement.

> Pandemics, which, according to Christ, will increase in number and ferocity at the end, will likely be used as another pretext for the suspension of what remains of the First Amendment.

Like Hitler, who emerged during an economic and political crisis, it will suspend any residual personal freedoms on the pretext of protecting national security and the common good. This rhetoric has greater appeal in the face of a military humiliation akin to that depicted in Daniel 11:29–32, which we'll examine later. Pandemics, which, according to Christ, will increase in number and ferocity at the end, will likely be used as another pretext for the suspension of what remains of the First Amendment.

Chapter 20

Lessons from the Rise of Hitler

Why did the Lord allow a single man, Adolf Hitler, over the course of about six years, to cause so much death and destruction? Was it to warn end-time Christians of the form the final antichrist will take?

As in Nazi Germany, which was controlled by the National Socialist Party, the world is being primed today by the social justice movement. This movement is essentially a front for the global destruction of Judeo-Christian values, the effect of which is to set the stage for humanity to accept another charismatic but ruthless tyrant. And as in Nazi Germany, I'm afraid most Christians, including Adventists, will accept the future antichrist like they did Hitler, who was blasphemously adored by all branches of the Christian German community with only a few exceptions.

It is a sad historical fact that most German Adventists in Hitler's day were complicit in his rise to power, in some cases by their silence and in others by their active betrayal to the authorities, leading to the deaths of their innocent brothers and sisters who were pacifists.

German Adventists failed to recognize the spirit of the antichrist in Hitler because, like him, they were carnally minded. Like most Western Adventists and Christians today, they were the moral products of their time—salt that had lost its savor. They had listened to and assimilated the culture around them rather than listening to and obeying the Word. This caused them to be attracted more to Hitler than to Christ and interpret prophecy by their own carnal minds.

As a Christian nation, Germany at this time suffered from the same superiority delusion as the Jews did in the days of Christ: the idea that they were the divinely favored, superior race. And this was rooted in the same spiritual disease that afflicts the end-time church of Laodicea: spiritual pride.

Another factor that tripped up German Adventists was that they, like Western Adventists do today, applied the prophecies of the mark of the beast too narrowly: to only the issue of Sunday versus Sabbath sacredness. I suggest that there were clear signs Hitler was an antichrist, but since German Adventists were focused on the letter of the law and not the Spirit animating it, they couldn't see Nazism for what it was.

However, the most important root cause of blindness among German Christians was failure to follow the golden rule (see Matt. 7:12). They did not put themselves in their neighbors shoes.

Like most Adventists today, the Adventists of Hitler's Germany believed the Sabbath would be an issue well before probation closed for all Germans. However, Ellen White said that while Sabbath observance will be a central issue, it does not become a global issue of life and death until near the close of probation, when Satan impersonates Christ (see *The Great Controversy*, p, 624ff).

Since there were few signs on the horizon of the Sabbath becoming an issue under Hitler for non-Jews, German Adventists were in denial. After all, wasn't the great *Führer* a vegetarian, and didn't he condone *their* worshiping on the Sabbath? The six million Sabbath-keeping Jews who were annihilated was an inconvenient fact they willfully chose to ignore. Hitler's approval rating remained high. Amazingly, it remained high in that generation well after the war, when the evil of Hitler's character was fully exposed. The delusion of Nazism was a permanent state for many.

Unfortunately, the same willful blindness is rampant today in Western Christianity and Adventism, which is why current and past church and political leaders have responded in silence or, at times, with approval of another genocide, that of the unborn, and why they have sat idly by during the suppression of freedoms that were narrowly preserved from the Nazis two generations ago by the blood of millions.

Many of our leaders have watched as our liberties have been eroded and removed over the last three decades, especially since 9/11 and particularly during the COVID pandemic. It took the humble Canadian truckers to help turn the tide. The February 2022 Canadian trucker protests of government overreach got the attention of the world. While I don't endorse the truckers' violation of municipal bylaws and acknowledge they made life more difficult for those living close to the protest site, I fully support their cause. If our religious and political leaders, who ought to know better, remain silent or actively endorse complicity much longer, like German Christians and Adventists did under Hitler, the results will be the same, but this time, it will be the free Western world that morphs into freedom's and Christ's worst enemy.

Let's face this issue for what it is and come to grips with the fact that the Battle of Armageddon, that great spiritual battle and the climax of the controversy between the forces of good and evil, is essentially already well underway and will only intensify from here onward until the beast is defeated and thrown alive, with the dragon and the false prophet, into the lake of fire. There's no going back now. With the Red Sea in front and the armies of Egypt behind, the Lord is calling us to move forward with Him right to the victorious return of Christ. The question is, Are we finally ready to willingly, gladly obey Him?

Considering what's been said, who or what exactly is the antichrist? We've reviewed several of his characteristics already, but in order to help us precisely identify it, we'll turn now to the prophecies of Daniel.

Chapter 21

The King of the North[V]

Inspiration indicates that the final verses of Daniel 11 are a road map for us:

> Soon the scenes of trouble spoken of in the prophecies will take place. The prophecy in the eleventh of Daniel has nearly reached its complete fulfillment. Much of the history that has taken place in fulfillment of this prophecy will be repeated. In the thirtieth verse a power is spoken of that "shall be grieved, and return, and have indignation against the holy covenant: so shall he do; he shall even return, and have intelligence with them that forsake the holy covenant." (White, *Manuscript Releases*, vol. 13, p. 394)

This prophecy was initially fulfilled in AD 538, when the Roman emperor Justinian "had intelligence with them that forsake the holy covenant." At this time, he granted civil power to the bishop of Rome as the corrector of heretics. The state fornicated with the church to force the conscience of worshipers, creating the abomination of desolation. The prophecy, however, applies preeminently to the end-times.

How do we know this? Following AD 538, the faithful followers of Christ were not able to take a clear, decided stand in favor of the gospel, and as a result, the world was enveloped in the shadows of the Dark Ages. For 1,000 years, the true church was sheltered in the wilderness while the truth languished under the rubbish of superstition and false doctrine until, in the fourteenth and fifteenth centuries, God began to raise up the great reformers—the heralds of the Reformation, such as Wycliffe, Huss, and Jerome.

However, when similar events occur in the future, it will be a different matter; the people of God "will be strong and do notable exploits" (Dan. 11: 32). Outwardly, they will still appear to be on the losing side; they will be driven into the wilderness, first politically, socially, and economically, and then finally, literally; but unlike the Waldensians, as the latter rain is poured out, they will bear a convincing testimony to the truth that will encircle the globe (see Rev 12:6).

Speaking of that time, Habakkuk testified that the world "shall be full of the knowledge of the glory of the LORD, as the waters cover the sea" (2:14). Thank God, the church will arise to the occasion to resist the devil's assaults. Through the church militant, God will give the last gospel message of mercy and warning to the world in latter-rain power.

During this time, we are told the church will be tried and purified yet endure to the end: "And some of them of understanding shall fall, to try them, and to purge, and to make them white, even to the time of the end" (Dan. 11:35).

This is the critical period of being made white—of the blotting out of sin in God's people: "because it is yet for a time appointed. And the king shall do according to his will; and he shall exalt himself, and magnify himself above every god, and shall speak marvelous things against the God of gods, and *shall prosper till the indignation be accomplished*: for that that is determined shall be done" (verses 35, 36, emphasis added).

When is this indignation accomplished? From other Bible passages, we know the indignation reaches its climax and fulfillment in the slaying of the two witnesses, a symbol for the deadly intolerance exercised against God's people. Their slaying will be literal and spiritual. Physically, some will die as martyrs. Spiritually, all will be silenced by the rejection of their testimony against the beast.

God warns humanity against taking this last fatal step:

And the third angel followed them, saying with a loud voice, If any man worship the beast and his image, and receive his mark in his forehead, or in his hand, The same shall drink of the wine of the wrath of God, which is poured out without mixture into the cup of his indignation; and he shall be tormented with fire and brimstone in the presence of the holy angels, and in the presence of the Lamb: And the smoke of their torment ascendeth up for ever and ever: and they have no rest day nor night, who worship the beast and his image, and whosoever receiveth the mark of his name. Here is the patience of the saints: here are they that keep the commandments of God, and the faith of Jesus. (Revelation 14:9–12)

The Beast and the King of the North

Historically, Babylon was the northern enemy of Israel. At the end, spiritual Babylon is also the main enemy of God's people. Some Christians view literal Israel as the target of the beast and Babylon. While it is quite true that the devil would like nothing better than to destroy the Jews—the Holocaust is evidence of this—he is actually more enraged and threatened by spiritual Israel, those who stand in direct opposition to him: "And the dragon was wroth with the woman, and went to make war with the remnant of her seed, which keep the commandments of God, and have the testimony of Jesus Christ" (Rev. 12:17).

Understanding this clarifies what it means in Daniel 11 when the King of the North invades the "glorious land" and pitches his tent "between the seas in the glorious holy mountain" (verse 45, LITV). In my view, this is another figure for the slaying of the two witnesses.

In the prophecies, beasts are used to describe kingdoms. In Daniel 7, there is a series of four beasts that depict the major empires of the world from Daniel's time to the return of Christ. Whereas the first three beasts are normal animals, albeit with unusual features (lion, bear, and leopard), the fourth and last beast, symbolic of Rome because of its unprecedented, barbaric cruelty, is represented by a monstrous beast, more ferocious and cruel than any found in nature.

In Revelation 13, the final beast of Daniel 7 is represented in two manifestations: the beast itself and the lamb-like beast that makes war on the saints and the Lamb by requiring all to worship a false God, the image of the first beast. Thankfully, God only permits this for its allotted time, and in the end, the image of the beast is swiftly conquered and destroyed by Christ.

In Daniel 11, we have the same picture of the apostasy and swift destruction of the King of the North, a parallel symbol of the same image beast that is erected and empowered by the lamb-like beast, spiritual Babylon. I believe the King of the North is the fourth beast of Daniel 7 and the image beast of Revelation 13 because he does the same acts; he makes war on the saints, the holy covenant, and the glorious land:

> He [the King of the North] shall ... have indignation against the holy covenant: so shall he do; he shall even return, and have intelligence

with them that forsake the holy covenant. And arms shall stand on his part, and they shall pollute the sanctuary of strength, and shall take away the daily sacrifice, and they shall place the abomination that maketh desolate. And such as do wickedly against the covenant shall he corrupt by flatteries: but the people that do know their God shall be strong, and do exploits. (Daniel 11:30–32)

The event described above marks the ascendancy of the lamb-like beast of Revelation 13 onto the world stage when it bids the world to make an image to the first beast. Here is my amplification of the preceding verses:

At the time appointed [the time of the end] he [the King of the North, a symbol of the lamb-like beast, the USA] shall return and come into the south [against the anti-Western powers—that is, Communism and post-Communism and Islam], but it shall not be this time as it was before [that is, it will not be the same this time as it was at the close of other wars when America returned home with wealth and honor]. For ships of Kittim shall come against him, and he [the lamb-like beast] shall be afraid and withdraw, and shall turn back and be enraged and take action against the holy covenant. He shall turn back and pay attention to those who forsake the holy covenant. (Daniel 11:29, 30, ESV)

The above passage describes a major economic and naval humiliation or threat that causes the US to back down from an all-out conflict with the King of the South. "Ships of Kittim" refers not only to war ships but merchant ships because ancient Kittim (modern Cyprus) was a hub for the merchants surrounding the Mediterranean Sea . Kittim is therefore a symbol of the international merchants and powers of Europe and western Asia that will oppose American policy and military involvement in the nations surrounding the Mediterranean. However, rather than humbling themselves before God, the leaders of America turn against Him and those who honor His covenant, the Ten Commandments.

The King of the North's "action against the holy covenant" describes the suspension of the First Amendment in America, which paves the way for the persecution of those who remain loyal to the covenant. This is the appearance of the abomination of desolation that marks the start of final events described in Daniel 8, 9, 11, and 12.

To human wisdom, it seems unlikely that the powers of Europe, some of America's closest allies, would become hostile to the US, but in my view,

> *To human wisdom, it seems unlikely that the powers of Europe, some of America's closest allies, would become hostile to the US, but in my view, this is what the prophecy is saying. And with the recent US sabotage of the Nord Stream natural gas pipeline, it has become more plausible.*

this is what the prophecy is saying. And with the recent US sabotage of the Nord Stream natural gas pipeline, it has become more plausible.

To summarize, beginning in Daniel 11:30, the King of the North is the USA because it best matches the lamb-like power of Revelation 13 that leads the earth to make and worship an image to the first beast by having "intelligence with those who forsake the holy covenant." I suggest an American military reversal and humiliation will be the motivating force that drives US leadership to ally with those who forsake the covenant to suspend the First Amendment. This marks the initial formation of the image of the beast.

I will close this chapter by referring you back to the beginning of it: Ellen White's timely commentary on Daniel 11:30.

Chapter 22

The Strange God of Forces

Earlier, I noted that the King of the North continues his rule until the "indignation is accomplished" (Dan. 11:36). Starting in verse 29, the world wonders after the beast and the image of it, but in verses 36–45, we have a transition to the final phase of the eighth head of Revelation 17:

> And the king shall do according to his will; and he shall exalt himself, and *magnify himself above every god*, and shall speak marvelous things against the God of gods, and *shall prosper till the indignation be accomplished*: for that that is determined shall be done. Neither shall he regard the God of his fathers, nor the desire of women, *nor regard any god*: for he shall magnify himself above all. But in his estate shall he honor *the God of forces*: and a god whom his fathers knew not shall he honor with gold, and silver, and with precious stones, and pleasant things. *Thus shall he do in the most strong holds with a strange god*, whom he shall acknowledge and increase with glory: and he shall cause them to rule over many, and shall divide the land for gain. (Daniel 11:36–39, emphasis added)

The above passage gives us several unique, identifying features of the antichrist. Verses 36 and 37 highlight a new kind of idolatry. The same traits of self-exaltation and the suppression of other forms of heathen idolatry and Christian worship are attributed to the man of sin: "Let no one deceive you by any means; for that Day will not come unless the falling away comes first, and the man of sin is revealed, the son of perdition, who opposes and exalts himself above all that is called God or that is worshiped

[Christian or heathen], so that he sits as God in the temple of God, *showing himself that he is God*" (2 Thess. 2:3, 4, NKJV, emphasis added).

This antichrist goes beyond what the popes ever claimed. Whereas the popes have made many outlandish, blasphemous claims to be the vicar of Christ, the prophecy indicates that at the end, this is taken to its ultimate conclusion. This demonic character claims to be the glorified Christ Himself.

This is the most dramatic, alarming feature of the antichrist and the surest identifier: While impersonating Christ, he actually rejects Him and the God of his fathers and, like Nebuchadnezzar, requires the worship of himself above all other gods on the pain of death. "Neither shall he regard the God of his fathers, nor the desire of women, *nor regard any god*: for he shall magnify himself above all" (Dan. 11:37, emphasis added).

Muslims have been expecting their messiah for centuries. To them, he will be the twelfth Mahdi; to Christians, the victorious Jesus; to Buddhists, Maitreya; to Hindus, Kalki; to Taoists, Li Hong; etc. But there's more. The phrase "god of forces" indicates this antichrist backs his claims to worship with overawing displays of supernatural power. Messiah-like, he will do great wonders. To most, it will be a convincing show. The prophecies state that America and the world will fall for his deceptions and acknowledge him as god.

> And he doeth great wonders, so that he maketh fire come down from heaven on the earth in the sight of men, And deceiveth them that dwell on the earth by the means of those miracles which he had power to do in the sight of the beast; saying to them that dwell on the earth, that they should make an image to the beast, which had the wound by a sword, and did live. And he had power to give life unto the image of the beast, that the image of the beast should both speak, and cause that as many as would not worship the image of the beast should be killed. (Revelation 13:13–15)

Like Hitler, he will promise prosperity and order. He will heal the sick and comfort the poor, but he will soon show his true colors by his policy against all who oppose him. Yet in spite of his demonic character, America, bedazzled by his outward splendor and the undeniable evidence of a supernatural power at work in him, will accept him as the glorified Christ. "And he causeth all, both small and great, rich and poor, free and bond, to receive a mark in their right hand, or in their foreheads: Here is wisdom. Let him that hath understanding count the number of the beast:

for it is the number of a man; and his number is Six hundred threescore and six" (verses 16–18).

With all that said, how do we know this antichrist is the *final* antichrist (refer to endnote v)? Because this one "shall prosper till the indignation be accomplished." This is the power that executes the final indignation—the final assault on the people of God. The evil of this abomination calls down the wrath of God unmingled with mercy on the beast and his image.

Armageddon

This brings us to Daniel 11:40–45, a vivid scene of armed conflict. A primary rule of prophetic interpretation is that all of Scripture should be understood literally unless there is clear reason to apply a symbolic meaning. Here, we have a future global conflict between the King of the North, the US, and the King of the South, it's enemies.

> And at the time of the end shall the king of the south push at him: and the king of the north shall come against him like a whirlwind, with chariots, and with horsemen, and with many ships; and he shall enter into the countries, and shall overflow and pass over.... *But tidings out of the east and out of the north shall trouble him:* therefore he shall go forth with great fury to destroy, and utterly to make away many. And he shall plant the tabernacles of his palace between the seas in the glorious holy mountain; yet he shall come to his end, and none shall help him. (Daniel 11:40, 44, 45, emphasis added).

This happened to a limited extent at 9/11, when Islamic extremists "pushed" the US and its allies, who responded with overwhelming force. It will happen on a much larger scale in the future and include the kings of the east, China, and Russia. "And the sixth angel poured out his vial upon the great river Euphrates; and the water thereof was dried up, that the way of the kings of the east might be prepared" (Rev. 16:12).

A new element is introduced in verses 41–45 as the conflict broadens to include the glorious land, the end-time church. To many Christians, the phrase "glorious land" refers to literal Israel, and that application should not be ruled out. However, the church, spiritual Israel, should be primarily understood here because, after the cross, the Old Testament prophecies regarding Israel apply primarily to spiritual Jews and spiritual Israel.

This is critical to keep straight in our minds because the spiritual aspect of the conflict is the essence of Armageddon; it is *the* great final battle for human souls. Although this includes a physical battle between the nations of the earth, this spiritual war, which takes place during the sixth and seventh plagues, is the essence of it:

> And the sixth angel poured out his vial upon the great river Euphrates; and the water thereof was dried up, that the way of the kings of the east might be prepared. And I saw three unclean spirits like frogs come out of the mouth of the dragon, and out of the mouth of the beast, and out of the mouth of the false prophet. For they are the spirits of devils, working miracles, which go forth unto the kings of the earth and of the whole world, to gather them to the battle of that great day of God Almighty. Behold, I come as a thief. Blessed is he that watcheth, and keepeth his garments, lest he walk naked, and they see his shame. And he gathered them together into a place called in the Hebrew tongue Armageddon. And the seventh angel poured out his vial into the air; and there came a great voice out of the temple of heaven, from the throne, saying, It is done. And there were voices, and thunders, and lightnings; and there was a great earthquake, such as was not since men were upon the earth, so mighty an earthquake, and so great. And the great city was divided into three parts, and the cities of the nations fell: and great Babylon came in remembrance before God, to give unto her the cup of the wine of the fierceness of his wrath. And every island fled away, and the mountains were not found. And there fell upon men a great hail out of heaven, every stone about the weight of a talent: and men blasphemed God because of the plague of the hail; for the plague thereof was exceeding great. (Revelation 16:12–21)

In Armageddon, the main protagonists are the true and false Elijahs—the true and false churches of the end. This deadly conflict between true and counterfeit religion has been fought from the time Cain slew Abel to when Ahab sought to slay Elijah and Christ was slain by His own people. This history will be repeated at the end of time as well.

However, we can thank God, the "glorious holy mountain," spiritual Mount Zion, describes the *purified* church that comes out of great tribulation gloriously triumphant. Babylon, that jealous harlot, eagerly attempts to destroy the pure woman, but the King of the North, spiritual Babylon, "shall come to his end and none shall help him" (Dan. 11:45).[vi]

Through this ordeal, the church is purified and made white. The church becomes the glorious bride of Christ.

Let's look now at some Armageddon statements from Ellen White confirming that the battle is primarily spiritual:

> The Battle of Armageddon will be fought. And that day must find none of us sleeping. Wide awake we must be, as wise virgins having oil in our vessels with our lamps. The power of the Holy Ghost must be upon us and the Captain of the Lord's host will stand at the head of the angels of heaven to direct the battle. Solemn events before us are yet to transpire. Trumpet after trumpet is to be sounded; vial after vial poured out one after another upon the inhabitants of the earth. Scenes of stupendous interest are right upon us and these things will be sure indications of the presence of Him who has directed in every aggressive movement, who has accompanied the march of His cause through all the ages, and who has graciously pledged Himself to be with His people in all their conflicts to the end of the world. He will vindicate His truth. He will cause it to triumph. He is ready to supply His faithful ones with motives and power of purpose, inspiring them with hope and courage and valor in increased activity as the time is at hand. (White, *Selected Messages*, book 3, p. 426)

> The Battle of Armageddon is soon to be fought. He on whose vesture is written the name, King of kings and Lord of lords, leads forth the armies of heaven on white horses, clothed in fine linen, clean and white. (White, *The SDA Bible Commentary*, vol. 7, p. 982)

> Every form of evil is to spring into intense activity. Evil angels unite their powers with evil men, and as they have been in constant conflict and attained an experience in the best modes of deception and battle, and have been strengthening for centuries, they will not yield the last great final contest without a desperate struggle. All the world will be on one side or the other of the question. The Battle of Armageddon will be fought, and that day must find none of us sleeping. Wide awake we must be, as wise virgins having oil in our vessels with our lamps. (White, *Maranatha*, p. 257)

> The present is a solemn, fearful time for the church. The angels are already girded, awaiting the mandate of God to pour their vials of wrath upon the world. Destroying angels are taking up the work of vengeance;

for the Spirit of God is gradually withdrawing from the world. Satan is also mustering his forces of evil, going forth "unto the kings of the earth and of the whole world," to gather them under his banner, to be trained for "the battle of that great day of God Almighty." Satan is to make most powerful efforts for the mastery in the last great conflict. Fundamental principles will be brought out, and decisions made in regard to them. Skepticism is prevailing everywhere. Ungodliness abounds. The faith of individual members of the church will be tested as though there were not another person in the world. (White, *The SDA Bible Commentary*, vol. 7, p. 983)[vii]

Chapter 23

The Seventh Plague

We need to study the pouring out of the seventh vial. The powers of evil will not yield up the conflict without a struggle. But Providence has a part to act in the Battle of Armageddon. When the earth is lighted with the glory of the angel of Revelation 18, the religious elements, good and evil, will awake from slumber, and the armies of the living God will take the field.

Ellen White, Manuscript Releases, vol. 19, p. 160

Let's now look briefly at the pouring out of the seventh vial, which inspiration links to the victory of Christ in the Battle of Armageddon:

> And he gathered them together into a place called in the Hebrew tongue Armageddon. And the seventh angel poured out his vial into the air; and there came a great voice out of the temple of heaven, from the throne, saying, It is done. And there were voices, and thunders, and lightnings; and there was a great earthquake, such as was not since men were upon the earth, so mighty an earthquake, and so great. And the great city was divided into three parts, and the cities of the nations fell: and great Babylon came in remembrance before God, to give unto her the cup of the wine of the fierceness of his wrath. (Revelation 16:16–19)

In the passage above, we have the following sequence: The nations are gathered together at Armageddon, the seventh vial is poured into the air, a great voice from the temple in heaven says, "It is done," and finally, an earthquake, literal and/or symbolic, divides the great city, Babylon, into three parts, and the cities of the nations fall. We know the "great city" in verse 19 is Babylon because she is called that in Revelation seven times directly and twice indirectly (see 11:8; 14:8; 16:19; 17:18; 18:10, 16, 18, 19, 21).

The counterpart to the seventh vial or plague is the seventh trumpet, which also announces the overthrow of all earthly kingdoms led by Babylon and their delivery into Christ's hand:

> And the seventh angel sounded; and there were great voices in heaven, saying, The kingdoms of this world are become the kingdoms of our Lord, and of his Christ; and he shall reign for ever and ever.... And the temple of God was opened in heaven, and there was seen in his temple the ark of his testament: and there were lightnings, and voices, and thunderings, and an earthquake, and great hail. (Revelation 11:15–19).

Regarding the seventh vial being poured into the air, this plague apparently corrupts the atmosphere. Since the seventh trumpet states that God will destroy those who destroy the earth, it seems like the seventh plague on the atmosphere is caused by human activity, possibly the result of biological warfare and/or radioactive fallout from nuclear war.

> " Since the seventh trumpet states that God will destroy those who destroy the earth, it seems like the seventh plague on the atmosphere is caused by human activity, possibly the result of biological warfare and/or radioactive fallout from nuclear war. "

Most significantly, the geopolitical consequence of Armageddon is that Babylon is overthrown, divided into three parts and burned with fire. Why three parts? Because Babylon is an alliance of three entities: the fallen church represented by the harlot, the state represented by the beast she rides, and spiritualism represented by the false prophet. When the kingdoms of the earth are given to Christ, He defeats these three components of Babylon and throws them into the lake of fire:

> And I saw heaven opened, and behold a white horse; and he that sat upon him [was] called Faithful and True, and in righteousness he doth judge and make war.... And I saw the beast, and the kings of the earth, and their armies, gathered together to make war against him that sat on the horse, and against his army. And the beast was taken, and with him the false prophet that wrought miracles before him, with which he deceived them that had received the mark of the beast, and them that worshipped his image. *These both were cast alive into a lake of fire*

burning with brimstone. And the remnant were slain with the sword of him that sat upon the horse, which [sword] proceeded out of his mouth: and all the fowls were filled with their flesh. (Revelation 19:11, 19–21, emphasis added)

Propaganda versus Truth

Armageddon is both a literal and spiritual battle. Spiritually, it is an information war. Propaganda wars are already raging all around us and will intensify, but consider this: For the world, the latter rain and the judgment of the living[13] are inseparable; the latter rain is the means of enlightenment that defeats propaganda, and judgment is the result. Human decisions regarding fundamental principles of right and wrong will be made.

The latter rain is the revelation of the glory of God—of the truth regarding His character that calls the world to account and defeats its propaganda. This is why the first angel can announce with the full authority of heaven that the "hour of His judgment is come." This is where the battle is engaged, and Christ as Commander of the hosts leads His invincible army onto the field.

---

[13] As was pointed out earlier, those who understand the ministry of Christ in the Holiest have been in the judgment of the living since they accepted that truth. For them, the "hour of his judgment [and atonement] is come." However, at a certain point, called "the times of the Gentiles," this judgment expands to include the rest of mankind (see Luke 21:24; Rev. 11:2).

Chapter 24

When Michael Stands Up

And at that time shall Michael stand up, the great prince which standeth for the children of thy people: and there shall be a time of trouble, such as never was since there was a nation even to that same time: and at that time thy people shall be delivered, every one that shall be found written in the book.

Daniel 12:1

In this chapter, we'll look at what happens when Michael, the Prince of the covenant, stands up. Some Christians, such as Adventists, teach that He stands at the close of probation. Ellen White made many statements supporting that position, but she also made others indicating He stands up before then. Below are two of her extraordinary statements, the first on Michael standing up at the start of the latter rain and the second on the Battle of Armageddon:

Daniel is today standing in his lot, and we are to give him place to speak to the people. Our message is to go forth as a lamp that burneth. "At that time shall Michael stand up, the great prince which standeth for the children of thy people: and there shall be a time of trouble, such as never was since there was a nation even to that same time: and at that time thy people shall be delivered, every one that shall be found written in the book. And many of them that sleep in the dust of the earth shall awake, some to everlasting life, and some to shame and everlasting contempt. And they that be wise shall shine as the brightness of the firmament; and they that turn many to righteousness as the stars forever and ever."

These words present the work that we are to do in these last days. We are not one-half awake. We have not the power that is essential to the doing of the work that must be done. We must come into life, come into union. Now, just now, we must stand in that position where repentance and pardon shall be the striking features of our work. There must be no quarreling. It is too late to engage with Satan in his work of blinding eyes. It is too late to give heed to seducing spirits and doctrines of devils.

I am instructed to say that when the Holy Spirit gives tongue and utterance, we shall see a work done similar to that done on the day of Pentecost. The representatives of Christ will work intelligently. There will not be found one man here and another there seeking to tear down and destroy. (White, *Australian Union Conference Record*, March 11, 1907)

In this second statement, mark how White also linked Armageddon to the latter rain, the midnight cry, and the sounding of the trumpets:

The Battle of Armageddon will be fought. And that day must find none of us sleeping. Wide awake we must be, as wise virgins having oil in our vessels with our lamps. The power of the Holy Ghost must be upon us and the Captain of the Lord's host will stand at the head of the angels of heaven to direct the battle. Solemn events before us are yet to transpire. Trumpet after trumpet is to be sounded; vial after vial poured out one after another upon the inhabitants of the earth. Scenes of stupendous interest are right upon us and these things will be sure indications of the presence of Him who has directed in every aggressive movement, who has accompanied the march of His cause through all the ages, and who has graciously pledged Himself to be with His people in all their conflicts to the end of the world. He will vindicate His truth. He will cause it to triumph. He is ready to supply His faithful ones with motives and power of purpose, inspiring them with hope and courage and valor in increased activity as the time is at hand. (White, *Selected Messages*, book 3, p. 426)

It is the latter rain that sparks Armageddon and results in 1) the enlightenment of the world, 2) the cleansing of the church, which is called out of Babylon, and 3) the church's sealing by the Prince of the covenant. Christ's cleansing of the temple was a type of that time when He rises to cleanse and seal the church, and according to Revelation 7, the sealing involves numbering.

Numbering Israel Anciently and Today

Under Mosaic law, census-taking was lawful, provided a half shekel of silver was paid for the ransom of every male numbered (see Exod. 30:12, 13). The requirement was symbolic of the end-times, when God numbers and ransoms the armies of spiritual Israel. The law stated that the purpose of the ransom was to prevent a plague from God on Israel. Similarly, in the last days, the hosts who are numbered and sealed by God are sheltered from the plagues that scourge all who receive the mark of the beast.

Israel was numbered as a nation for the first time one year after the Exodus, shortly after the tabernacle was built.

> And the LORD spake unto Moses in the wilderness of Sinai, in the tabernacle of the congregation, on the first day of the second month, in the second year after they were come out of the land of Egypt, saying, Take ye the sum of all the congregation of the children of Israel, after their families, by the house of their fathers, with the number of their names, every male by their polls. (Numbers 1:1, 2)

The record states that all the tribes were numbered at this time, except Levi. Shortly after this, Levi was numbered separately, and at the same time, the firstborn from every tribe were also numbered because the Lord was going to do an exchange. He had hallowed all of Israel's firstborn to Himself when He killed the firstborn of the Egyptians while passing over the families of Israel. In the place of the firstborn to minister as priests, the Lord selected the men of Levi. The number of the men of Levi was taken and found to be 273 less than the number of the firstborn men of Israel (see chapter 3).

God accepted the Levites in the place of the firstborn, but to make up the 273-man difference, the firstborn who were in excess of the Levites were ransomed for five shekels each, ten times the redemption price of the regular Israelites during a census. That should have been more than enough evidence for Korah, a Levite, of how highly the Lord valued the services of his tribe, but he was not content with the Lord's valuation. He, along with Dathan and Abiram, Reubenites, wanted it all. They coveted the leadership of Moses and the priesthood of Aaron (see chapter 16).

Forty years later, a second census was taken. This one had two purposes: 1) to verify that all of the previous generation had died to fulfill the oath of God that none of them would enter the Promised Land; and 2) to be used in allotting the land of Canaan fairly, giving each tribe an amount of land according to its population, but with the provision that the land was still to be divided by the Lord by lot.

> These were the numbered of the children of Israel, six hundred thousand and a thousand seven hundred and thirty. And the LORD spake unto Moses, saying, Unto these the land shall be divided for an inheritance according to the number of names. To many thou shalt give the more inheritance, and to few thou shalt give the less inheritance: to every one shall his inheritance be given according to those that were numbered of him. Notwithstanding the land shall be divided by lot: according to the names of the tribes of their fathers they shall inherit. According to the lot shall the possession thereof be divided between many and few. (Numbers 26:51–56)

At this census, the Levites were numbered separately from Israel again and not counted with the rest because, as a tribe, they were not given their own territory as an inheritance. Instead, they were given the priesthood and forty-eight cities scattered throughout Israel.

There is no record of Israel ever disobeying the census requirement until we come to the reign of King David. At his command, the provisions of the law were not followed, and God did indeed plague the nation for three days. This history has several interesting parallels to the numbering of spiritual Israel, the 144,000, and the time of Jacob's trouble (see 1 Chron. 21).

The account of David's sin begins with Satan standing up against Israel, like he does in Zechariah 3 and will do at the end. He provoked David to number the nation without the required redemption money. Joab, David's commander, protested against the plan, warning the king of the consequences, but David was dismissive. Perhaps one reason Joab's warning fell on deaf ears is he did not refer to the redemption requirement. David was probably well aware of it. He may have rationalized that the redemption money was not required because this was a census of fighting men, not a census of the nation.

However, David's action compounded the sin. A national census of the men was lawful, but there was no provision in the law for a census of the fighting men. Such a census demonstrated a lack of faith in divine protection. It mirrored the trust in human and military might of the surrounding heathen nations.

As soon as Joab returned with the tally, the Lord sent the prophet Gad to rebuke David and required him to choose the punishment: three years of famine, three months of defeat at the hands of his enemies, or three days of plague. David wisely chose to fall "into the hand of the Lord" rather than "into the hand of man" (1 Chron. 21:13).

The plague immediately began and ravaged Israel, killing 70,000 men. On the third day of the plague, an angel stood with a drawn sword over Jerusalem by the threshing floor of Ornan the Jebusite (see verse 15). God through Gad instructed David to build an altar there, that the plague might be stayed and Jerusalem might be saved. The land belonging to Ornan was Mount Moriah. It had been divinely allotted to Judah when Israel was numbered at the start of the conquest of Canaan, but over 400 years later, it was still owned by a Jebusite, one of the nations Israel was commanded to dispossess and destroy (see Exod. 32:2).

Before David could sacrifice an offering there, he needed to obtain the land. The owner, Ornan, may have understood that he had no right in the land because God had given it to Israel. The Jebusite offered it to the king at no charge, but David gave him the full price of it, offered there as God had directed, and the plague was stopped.

> During the numbering of the 144,000, Satan stands up to accuse Israel, but the Angel rebukes and silences him. Israel is cleansed and clothed in the righteousness of Christ, sealed by the Holy Spirit and commissioned as priests and kings. The plagues cannot touch them, and they are sent out by Christ to tread on scorpions.

Notice the connection between numbering Israel, the plague, and the future temple site that God Himself selected: a threshing floor in active use. In Zechariah, when the Lord stands up as judge of all the living, there is a pause as the winds of strife are held back and spiritual Israel is numbered: "Be silent, O all flesh, before the LORD: for he is raised up out of his holy habitation" (2:13). During the numbering of the 144,000, Satan stands up to accuse Israel, but the Angel rebukes and silences him. Israel is cleansed and clothed in the righteousness of Christ, sealed by the Holy Spirit and commissioned as priests and kings. The plagues cannot touch them, and they are sent out by Christ to tread on scorpions (see Luke 10:19).

And he said unto me, It is done. I am Alpha and Omega, the beginning and the end. I will give unto him that is athirst of the fountain of the water of life freely. He that overcometh shall inherit all things; and I will be his God, and he shall be my son.

Revelation 21:6, 7

Chapter 25

Loma Linda and the Oath of Michael

And the angel ... lifted up his hand to heaven, And sware by him that liveth for ever and ever, who created heaven, and the things that therein are, and the earth, and the things that therein are, and the sea, and the things which are therein, that in the days of the voice of the seventh angel, when he shall begin to sound, the mystery of God should be finished, as he hath declared to his servants the prophets.

Revelation 10: 5–7

In 1906, two days before the Great San Francisco earthquake, while at Loma Linda, California, Ellen White had the following graphic night vision:

I stood on an eminence, from which I could see houses shaken like a reed in the wind. Buildings, great and small, were falling to the ground. Pleasure resorts, theaters, hotels, and the homes of the wealthy were shaken and shattered. Many lives were blotted out of existence, and the air was filled with the shrieks of the injured and the terrified.

The destroying angels of God were at work. One touch, and buildings, so thoroughly constructed that men regarded them as secure against every danger, quickly became heaps of rubbish. There was no assurance of safety in any place. I did not feel in any special peril, but the awfulness of the scenes that passed before me I cannot find words to describe. *It seemed that the forbearance of God was exhausted and that the Judgment day had come.*

The angel that stood at my side then instructed me that but few have any conception of the wickedness existing in our world today, and especially the wickedness in the large cities. He declared that the Lord has *appointed a time when He will visit transgressors in wrath for persistent disregard of His law.*

Terrible as was the representation that passed before me, that which impressed itself most vividly upon my mind was the instruction given in connection with it. *The angel that stood by my side declared that God's supreme rulership and the sacredness of His law must be revealed to those who persistently refused to render obedience to the King of kings....*

Throughout the following day I pondered the scenes that had passed before me and the instruction that had been given. During the afternoon we journeyed to Glendale, near Los Angeles; and the following night I was again instructed regarding the holiness and binding claims of the Ten Commandments and the supremacy of God above all earthly rulers....

On April 18, two days after the scene of falling buildings had passed before me, I went to fill an appointment in the Carr Street Church, Los Angeles. As we neared the church we heard the newsboys crying: "San Francisco destroyed by an earthquake!" With a heavy heart I read the first hastily printed news of the terrible disaster. (White, *Testimonies for the Church*, vol. 9, pp. 92–94, emphasis added)

Ellen White went on to apply the judgments found in Zephaniah 1 to her vision, but the above excerpt, especially the emphasized parts, are enough to show that what she saw in vision was not merely the 1906 San Francisco disaster but something greater still: judgment day. She reinforced this thought at the end of her account by warning of a mysterious "series of events" that will reveal that "God is master of the situation." Notice below that this chain of events doesn't announce the close of judgment and probation but rather its *beginning* and the latter rain:

God cannot forbear much longer. Already His judgments are beginning to fall on some places, and soon His signal displeasure will be felt in other places.

There will be a series of events revealing that God is master of the situation. The truth will be proclaimed in clear, unmistakable language. As a people we must prepare the way of the Lord under the overruling guidance of the Holy Spirit. The gospel is to be given in its purity. (White, *Testimonies for the Church*, vol. 9, p. 96, emphasis added)

Some may disagree with me here, but I believe this "series of events" is the thunderous announcement of the mighty Angel of Revelation 10, which demands the world's attention. This is followed by the same Angel's most solemn oath, but before looking more closely at the oath, we'll look briefly at another aspect of the vision. This is something that can easily be missed, but it may have an important application to Adventism in general and Loma Linda in particular.

Robert Olson, former director of the White Estate, observed that Ellen White was often on the scene when given a vision concerning that place, like she was in Nashville during her fireball vision. This one was at Loma Linda. She said, "It seemed that … judgment day had come." Judgment begins at the house of God (see 1 Peter 4:17), and this community, Loma Linda, is like Jerusalem to Adventists; it has the greatest concentration of Adventist wealth and talent. Speaking of the vision, she also said, "Through His prophet Zephaniah the Lord specifies the judgments that He will bring upon evildoers" and cited Zephaniah 1:8, indicating that God would punish the king's children, Adventists, not San Francisco.

Would God actually do something like that? When we run Him out of options, He sometimes has no other choice. He's done it twice to Jerusalem, which He loved, and twice to our institutions at Battle Creek, which He also loved, when they went off the rails.

In the fall of 2022, I discovered online several of Pastor Bill Lehman's sermons from the 1970s, when he was pastor of the Loma Linda Campus Hill Church, and I was impressed that the brethren tolerated him and allowed him to point out their sins. While there, he delivered an extended sermon series on the book *The Ministry of Healing* that is powerful and must have had an impact. Now, where is Loma Linda spiritually today? If we look at the university's handling of the pandemic, we see rebellion and trampling on conscience and real science for the gods of wealth, status, and ambition.

Returning to the connection between this "series of events" and Christ's oath in Revelation 10, Adventism was forged in the furnace of a great disappointment. On the day of the church's greatest grief, October 22, 1844, God restored to us our greatest blessing and hope: the completion of the new covenant in us. Like the revelation to Israel at Mount Sinai, God revealed Himself to our pioneers in the Most Holy Place of the heavenly sanctuary at that time. We discovered there at His throne *both* law and grace—justice and mercy—beautifully combined in the person of Christ—the Word, the Lord our Righteousness.

This is the reason for the existence of our prophetic movement. Our mission is nothing less than the global proclamation of the covenant—the writing of His law, Christ Our Righteousness, on our hearts so thoroughly and indelibly that our spiritual DNA is fully, totally restored (see Jer. 31:31–33; Heb. 8:6–13; 9:15; 10:16, 17; 12:24; 13:20).

In the early 1840s, the mighty Angel of Revelation 10, encircled by the covenant bow, commissioned Adventism to carry the Protestant Reformation forward to its conclusion, not so much by argument but by demonstration. The result was the second great awakening. At the end, the same Angel recommissions us at the start of the latter rain to "prophesy again" (verses 10, 11).

> The central issue in the great controversy between Christ and Satan is whether God can do what He says and do it so completely that, like the 70s TV character The Six Million Dollar Man, the redeemed person is "better than he was before"—not incrementally better but fundamentally transformed.

The central issue in the great controversy between Christ and Satan is whether God can do what He says and do it so completely that, like the 70s TV character The Six Million Dollar Man, the redeemed person is "better than he was before"—not incrementally better but fundamentally transformed. To help establish our faith that indeed He can transform us, as we're entering the final conflict, He reaffirms His promise with an oath, guaranteeing us complete liberation in Christ. Let's look more closely now at this oath and its history.

The Lord's Oath to Abraham

When Abraham was old and childless, the Lord promised him that all nations would be blessed through his seed. In response, Abraham believed God, and it was reckoned to him for righteousness (see Gen. 15:6). However, because giving birth to a son was a physical impossibility for Sarah, Abraham petitioned the Lord for a tangible sign that He would fulfill His word. The heart of God was moved at this request, and wanting to establish His friend's faith even more firmly (remember, Abraham already believed), the Lord condescended to supplement His promise with an oath given in the manner customary for those times. God solemnly passed between the parted animals, saying in symbol that on His very life, He would fulfill His promise.

Amazingly, in the last days, the Lord, knowing our weakness, condescends once again and does the same thing for us. And the results are similar: The oath is followed by the birth of the Child of promise, the Man-child who is caught up to the throne of God, where He is gloriously enthroned with more than Pentecostal authority and rules in the midst of His foes.

> And the dragon stood before the woman which was ready to be delivered, for to devour her child as soon as it was born. And she brought forth a man child, who was to rule all nations with a rod of iron: and her child was caught up unto God, and to his throne. (Revelation 12:4, 5)

> The LORD said unto my Lord, Sit thou at my right hand, until I make thine enemies thy footstool. The LORD shall send the rod of thy strength out of Zion: rule thou in the midst of thine enemies. (Psalm 110:1, 2)

At His second coronation, marked by the latter rain, our King, before His second advent, judges the fallen kingdoms of earth that confederate and league with the beast (see Rev. 12:5; Dan. 2:44, 45). It is He who by "a series of events reveal[s] that God is master of the situation."

Notice His posture, standing erect on behalf of spiritual Israel, with uplifted hand, taking the most solemn oath in the name of the Father:

> And the angel which I saw stand upon the sea and upon the earth lifted up his hand to heaven, And sware by him that liveth for ever and ever ... that there should be time no longer: But in the days of the voice of the seventh angel, when he shall begin to sound, *the mystery of God should be finished,* as he hath declared to his servants the prophets. (Revelation 10:5–7)

We know the above oath is extremely important to us because 1) Christ Himself makes it—He is the mighty Angel; and 2) He swears by none other than God. Christ rarely makes such an oath in Scripture. His oath to Abraham is the only one that comes close to this, and that oath was and still is very significant (see Heb. 6, 7).

However, this final one is greater still. Christ underlines its importance and exalts it even above His oath to Abraham in two ways: 1) by making it twice—once in Revelation 10 and once in Daniel 12; and 2) by sealing it in both cases, not, as in Abraham's day, with severed animals that flank Him on either side, but with two living witnesses of the redeemed on His right and left hands. Notice the position of the "man clothed in linen" and the two holy witnesses:

> Then I Daniel looked, and, behold, there stood other two, the one on this side of the bank of the river, and the other on that side of the bank of the river. And one said to the man clothed in linen, which was upon the waters of the river, How long shall it be to the end of these wonders? And I heard the man clothed in linen, which was upon the waters of the river, when he held up his right hand and his left hand unto heaven, and sware by him that liveth for ever that it shall be for a time, times, and an half; and when he shall have accomplished to scatter the power of the holy people, all these things shall be finished.... *Many shall be purified, and made white, and tried*; but the wicked shall do wickedly: and none of the wicked shall understand; but the wise shall understand. (Daniel 12:5–7, 10, emphasis added: see also Rev. 11; Zech. 4:3–14)

By His oath, Michael assures the church that before the end, the "mystery of God," Christ revealed in His people, will be fulfilled (see Rev. 10:7). "Many shall be purified, and made white."

Since my childhood, I've heard Adventist leaders and laymen both expressing their doubts that Christ can completely restore the divine image in fallen mortals this side of eternity. God has heard our faithless conversation, too, and it grieves Him, but He still loves us, and to better establish our trembling faith, He answers us with an oath.

Like the transfiguration, which greatly strengthened Christ to endure the cross, this oath is given to strengthen the remnant church before her final test (see Matt. 17:1–8; Luke 9:28–36). Therefore, we need to study it carefully and ingest it by faith so that, like Christ, we're also strengthened to endure the test and fulfill our commission to "prophesy again."

Notice how this oath is mirrored in Christ's transfiguration. In Daniel 12, Michael stands over the river, symbolic of the river of life, and on either side of Him is a witness: One, like Moses, represents those who have passed under the dominion of death but are raised by Christ, and the other, like Elijah, represents those who never come under the power of death but are translated.

By this figure, Michael reassures His people that in the final ordeal, live or die, on this side or that, none need to fear. He promises us under oath that there will indeed be a first-fruits harvest. These first fruits dispel all doubts about the power of Christ to save to the uttermost all who come unto God by Him (see Heb. 7:25). These are the manifest children of God whom all creation longs to see with an inexpressible desire, who, by their lives, magnify the power of God's love—a love stronger than sin and the grave (see Rom. 8:19).

Now notice also how the oath mirrors the first angel's message in 1) volume—it is loud; 2) extent—it is global; and 3) content—it points to our Creator God.

Just as the mighty Angel announced the first angel's message at the second great awakening, the same announcement is repeated at the end, but in latter rain power at the "hour of His judgment." When He stands up and utters the oath, His sheep will know it because they will recognize the Shepherd's voice. Like when the Greeks sought out Jesus in the temple just before His crucifixion, and He asked His Father to glorify His name, a voice came from heaven. A few standing by heard and understood the voice, but to most in that crowd, it sounded like muffled thunder. In the same way, when Michael rises to shake the earth, there will be lightning, thundering, voices, and an earthquake (see Rev. 4:5; 8:5; 11:19).

Today, on the eve of our final conflict, we have greater assurances than were given even to Abraham, the friend of God; we have the covenant promise confirmed by a double oath doubly witnessed.

The Day Before the Great San Francisco Earthquake

According to Ellen White, the historic San Francisco earthquake is a type of judgment day, but for the faithful, it is their wedding day. There are important clues in the 48 hours that transpired between her first vision and the earthquake that help us understand how this works. Between those two events, she had a second vision the night before the earthquake that is equally significant. The next paragraph gives the background for her second revelation:

> Terrible as was the representation that passed before me, that which impressed itself most vividly upon my mind was the instruction given in connection with it. The angel that stood by my side declared that God's supreme rulership and the sacredness of His law must be revealed to those who persistently refused to render obedience to the King of kings. *Those who choose to remain disloyal must be visited in mercy with judgments, in order that, if possible, they may be aroused to a realization*

of the sinfulness of their course. (White, *Testimonies for the Church*, vol. 9, p. 93, emphasis added)

Throughout the following day, White pondered the scenes that had passed before her the night before and the instruction that had been given. During the afternoon, she traveled to Glendale, near Los Angeles; and the following night, she was again instructed regarding the holiness and binding claims of the Ten Commandments and the supremacy of God above all earthly rulers:

> I seemed to be in an assembly, setting before the people the requirements of God's law. I read the scriptures regarding the institution of the Sabbath in Eden at the close of the creation week, and regarding the giving of the law at Sinai; and then declared that the Sabbath is to be observed "for a perpetual covenant" as a sign between God and His people forever, that they may know that they are sanctified by the Lord, their Creator.
>
> Then I further dwelt upon the supreme rulership of God above all earthly rulers. His law is to be the standard of action. Men are forbidden to pervert their senses by intemperance or by yielding their minds to satanic influences, for this makes impossible the keeping of God's law. While the divine Ruler bears long with perversity, He is not deceived and will not always keep silence. His supremacy, His authority as Ruler of the universe, must finally be acknowledged and the just claims of His law vindicated.
>
> Much more instruction regarding the long-sufferance of God and the necessity of arousing transgressors to a realization of their perilous position in His sight was repeated to the people, as received from my instructor.
>
> On April 18, two days after the scene of falling buildings had passed before me, I went to fill an appointment in the Carr Street Church, Los Angeles. As we neared the church we heard the newsboys crying: "San Francisco destroyed by an earthquake!" With a heavy heart I read the first hastily printed news of the terrible disaster.
>
> Two weeks later, on our homeward journey, we passed through San Francisco and, hiring a carriage, spent an hour and a half in viewing the destruction wrought in that great city. Buildings that were thought to be proof against disaster were lying in ruins. In some instances buildings were partially sunken in the ground. The city presented a most dreadful picture of the inefficiency of human ingenuity to frame

fireproof and earthquake-proof structures. (White, *Testimonies for the Church*, vol. 9, pp. 94, 95)

In the second revelation, I suggest White is a type of the recommissioned remnant who "prophesy again" after the seismic "sequence of events" begins to unfold. She represents those who obey the commission and explain to the people that, as traumatic as these judgments are, they are permitted by a God of love who is awakening and wooing His bride, pleading with her to flee Babylon and put on her beautiful garments, which He graciously supplies.

White then went on to confirm the scriptures that say judgment starts with the household of God:

Through His prophet Zephaniah the Lord specifies the judgments that He will bring upon evildoers:

"I will utterly consume all things from off the land, saith the Lord. I will consume man and beast; I will consume the fowls of the heaven, and the fishes of the sea, and the stumbling blocks with the wicked; and I will cut off man from off the land, saith the Lord."

"*And it shall come to pass in the day of the Lord's sacrifice, that I will punish the princes, and the king's children, and all such as are clothed with strange apparel.* In the same day also will I punish all those that leap on the threshold, which fill their masters' houses with violence and deceit....

"*And it shall come to pass at that time, that I will search Jerusalem with candles*, and punish the men that are settled on their lees: that say in their heart, The Lord will not do good, neither will He do evil. Therefore their goods shall become a booty, and their houses a desolation: they shall also build houses, but not inhabit them; and they shall plant vineyards, but not drink the wine thereof.

"The great day of the Lord is near, it is near, and hasteth greatly, even the voice of the day of the Lord: the mighty man shall cry there bitterly. That day is a day of wrath, a day of trouble and distress, a day of wasteness and desolation, a day of darkness and gloominess, a day of clouds and thick darkness, a day of the trumpet and alarm against the fenced cities, and against the high towers. And I will bring distress upon men, that they shall walk like blind men, because they have sinned against the Lord: and their blood shall be poured out as dust, and their flesh as the dung. Neither their silver nor their gold shall be able to deliver them in the day of the Lord's wrath; but the whole land shall be devoured by the fire of His jealousy: for He shall make even a speedy riddance of all them that dwell in the land." Zephaniah 1:2, 3, 8–18. (White, *Testimonies for the Church*, vol. 9, pp. 95, 96, emphasis added)

Finally, White closed with this pointed warning and beautiful description of the refreshing. In it, we can hear the Father's assurance, confirmed by an oath, that notwithstanding the initial pain and rude awakening, these are the days of courtship and marriage of His bride:

God cannot forbear much longer. Already His judgments are beginning to fall on some places, and soon His signal displeasure will be felt in other places.

There will be a series of events revealing that God is master of the situation. The truth will be proclaimed in clear, unmistakable language. As a people we must prepare the way of the Lord under the overruling guidance of the Holy Spirit. The gospel is to be given in its purity. The stream of living water is to deepen and widen in its course. In all fields, nigh and afar off, men will be called from the plow and from the more common commercial business vocations that largely occupy the mind, and will be educated in connection with men of experience. As they learn to labor effectively they will proclaim the truth with power. Through most wonderful workings of divine providence, mountains of difficulty will be removed and cast into the sea. The message that means so much to the dwellers upon the earth will be heard and understood. Men will know what is truth. Onward and still onward the work will advance until the whole earth shall have been warned, and then shall the end come. (White, *Testimonies for the Church*, vol. 9, p. 96)

Before leaving this topic, we need to look at one more related vision: the first one given to Ellen White when she was a tender youth of seventeen. In it, she saw the remnant who were toiling up a narrow, high path that led to the City of God. It was a taxing journey, and many of the travelers grew weary and discouraged. However, Jesus, who was at the end of the path, encouraged them "by raising His glorious right arm, and from His arm came a light which waved over the Advent band, and they shouted, 'Alleluia.'" This is the refreshing of the latter rain. And then the scene below comes next:

Soon we heard the voice of God like many waters, which gave us the day and hour of Jesus' coming. The living saints, 144,000 in number, knew and understood the voice, while the wicked thought it was thunder and an earthquake. *When God spoke the time, He poured upon us the Holy Ghost, and our faces began to light up and shine with the glory of God, as Moses' did when he came down from Mount Sinai.* (White, *Early Writings*, p. 14, emphasis added)

As I was studying this not long ago, what struck me was the idea that this scene announcing the time of Christ's return is the same as Michael announcing the oath towards the close of the latter rain (see Dan. 12; Rev. 10). This oath does at least two things: 1) Like in the early part of the latter rain, it completes the seal and empowers the remnant to endure the final test; and 2) it tells the remnant when the time periods in Daniel 12 end and Christ returns.

Just as Christ knew beforehand that He would lay down His life as the Passover Lamb on the literal day of Passover, so the remnant will know the time frame of their final test and deliverance. When God makes the announcement, they understand their final test is imminent because it occurs just before the return of Christ.

This implies that the starting point of the final three-and-a-half years of Daniel and Revelation may not be known until they are about to expire. That is consistent with statements by Ellen White that God's people will not have any further messages on time. For example, "This time, which the angel declares with a solemn oath, is not the end of this world's history, neither of probationary time, but of prophetic time, which should precede the advent of our Lord. That is, the people will not have another message upon definite time" (*The SDA Bible Commentary*, vol. 7, p. 971).

This agrees with Daniel 12, which says the wicked will not understand this vision or the time periods (see verse 10).

It is an awesome thought that God would promise, swearing by Himself to us, that there will be no more delay. He will return right at the appointed time for His bride.

> "Just as Christ knew beforehand that He would lay down His life as the Passover Lamb on the literal day of Passover, so the remnant will know the time frame of their final test and deliverance. When God makes the announcement, they understand their final test is imminent because it occurs just before the return of Christ."

Chapter 26

When Should We Pray for the Latter Rain?

The Lord Jesus, when He was here, spoke more about the Holy Spirit and our need to ask for Him than He did any other topic. The prophets of the Old Testament had a similar message: "Ask ye of the LORD rain in the time of the latter rain; *so* the LORD shall make bright clouds, and give them showers of rain, to every one grass in the field" (Zech. 10:1).

While we should always pray for the blessing and presence of the Spirit in our souls, in the above text, the Lord invites us, even urges us, to petition Him for the outpouring of His Spirit when it is needed most: at "the time of the latter rain." The verse implies that when the time comes for the Spirit to be given, those who understand the times will, like Daniel at the end of the seventy years prophesied by Jeremiah, earnestly petition God for the fulfillment of His promise.

Sacred history confirms that all the greatest acts of God are prefigured in the feasts of the Hebrew calendar. If the early rain, Pentecost, was prefigured then, how much more will the greater, end-time refreshing be foreshadowed in the feasts as well? The question is, Which feast points to it? In the following paragraphs, I make the case that the refreshing begins soon after the Day of Atonement, at the Feast of Ingathering, also called the Feast of Booths or Feast of Tabernacles. Let's now look at the Scriptures.

Thanks to Joel, we have the timing of the refreshing spelled out quite clearly, in black and white: "Be glad then, ye children of Zion, and rejoice in the LORD your God: for he hath given you the former rain moderately, and he will cause to come down for you the rain, the former rain, and the latter rain *in the first month*" (2:23, emphasis added).

The last word of this verse is not in the Hebrew manuscripts. "Month" has been supplied by the translators. Some English translations, such as the King James Version, point us to the beginning of the year, assuming it occurs on day 1 of the first Hebrew month. *Strong's Concordance* does the same, suggesting the term "latter rain" (Heb. *malqosh*) in Joel 2:23 refers to the "spring rain," but this is apparently incorrect as Strong himself noted that the word is derived from *laqash*, meaning "to gather the final crop," and *leqesh*, meaning "the final growth" or "after crop of the fall."

The likely reason for the mistake in both cases is that Strong and the translators of the KJV assumed the first of the year was in the spring in Israel. However, the Hebrew calendar has two beginnings: the first month, called Nisan, in the spring, and six months later, the start of the new year on the first day of the seventh month, called Tishri, in the fall.

This is consistent with the scriptural definition of the day, which begins in the evening with the fall of darkness followed by the daylight hours. Similarly, the year in Scripture starts with the darkness of the winter months, followed by the dawning of spring and the full day of summer.

The fall start of the year is further confirmed by the Sabbatical and Jubilee cycles, both of which start here (see Lev. 23:24, 25; 25:1–10).

Modern Jews hold this view as well. *Rosh Hashanah*, the Feast of Trumpets, is New Year's Day to the Jews. A new year that starts on the first day of the *seventh* month seems strange to us, but it is consistent with the Bible's chronology, which is based on the perfect number seven: the seven days of the week, the sabbaticals of seven years, and the Jubilees of seven sabbaticals are all reckoned by units of seven.

Regarding the Feast of Tabernacles, Zechariah ends with a divine imperative to all nations, not merely Jews, to keep this in the end times. Any person or nation that fails to do this will be plagued with a flesh-eating disease and receive no rain—the latter rain. Of course, this doesn't mean we are to reinstate this part of the ceremonial law; it means we must participate in the move of God at His appointed time, the Feast of Tabernacles:

> For I will gather all nations against Jerusalem to battle ... Then shall the LORD go forth, and fight against those nations, as when he fought in the day of battle.... And ye shall flee to the valley of my mountains; for the valley of the mountains shall reach unto Azal: yea, ye shall flee, like as ye fled from before the earthquake in the days of Uzziah king of Judah [a prophecy of the sixth seal where the Lord briefly discloses His

majesty to the unfaithful shepherd]: and the LORD my God shall come, and all the saints ones with thee.... But it shall be one day which shall be known unto the LORD; not day, nor night: but it shall come to pass, that at evening time it shall be light. And it shall be in that day, that living waters [the latter rain] shall go out from Jerusalem; half of them toward the former sea, and half of them toward the hinder sea ... And this shall be the plague wherewith the LORD will smite all the peoples that have fought against Jerusalem; Their flesh shall consume away while they stand upon their feet, and their eyes shall consume away in their holes, and their tongue shall consume away in their mouth.... And it shall come to pass, that every one that is left of all the nations which came against Jerusalem shall even go up from year to year to worship the King, the LORD of hosts, and to keep the feast of tabernacles. And it shall be, that whoso will not come up of all the families of the earth unto Jerusalem to worship the King, the LORD of hosts, even upon them shall be no rain [the latter rain]. And if the family of Egypt go not up, and come not, that have no rain; there shall be the plague, wherewith the LORD will smite the heathen that come not up to keep the feast of tabernacles. This shall be the punishment of Egypt, and the punishment of all nations that come not up to keep the feast of tabernacles. (Zechariah 14:2, 3, 5, 7, 8, 12, 16–19)

Linking the timing of the latter rain to the seventh month agrees with the prophecy that Christ read at the start of his ministry in Nazareth:

The Spirit of the Lord GOD *is* upon me; because the LORD hath anointed me to preach good tidings unto the meek; he hath sent me to bind up the brokenhearted, to proclaim liberty to the captives, and the opening of the prison to them that are bound; To proclaim the acceptable year of the LORD, and the day of vengeance of our God. (Isaiah 61:1, 2)

After Jesus read the above passage, except the last phrase, "and the day of vengeance of our God," Luke tells us He closed the book and sat down: "And the eyes of all them that were in the synagogue were fastened on him. And he began to say unto them, *This day is this scripture fulfilled in your ears*" (4:20, 21, emphasis added).

On what day did Christ read this? Was it at the beginning of the final sabbatical, the "acceptable year?" It seems so. Recall that according to Daniel 9, the Messiah would appear at the start of the final sabbatical, the 483rd of the 490 years (i.e., 70 weeks). Christ, in pointing to the "acceptable year," was saying the Spirit had been poured on Him that day to proclaim the final sabbatical of Daniel 9. And from that time forward, He and the disciples proclaimed the message, saying, "The time is fulfilled [referring to Daniel 9], the kingdom of God is at hand, repent and believe the gospel" (Mark 1:15).

Christ affirmed the connection of the outpouring of the Spirit with the Feast of Tabernacles three years later, near the close of His ministry:

> In the last day, that great day of the feast, Jesus stood and cried, saying, If any man thirst, let him come unto me, and drink. He that believeth on me, as the scripture hath said, out of his belly shall flow rivers of living water. (*But this spake he of the Spirit, which they that believe on him should receive: for the Holy Ghost was not yet given; because that Jesus was not yet glorified.*) (John 7:37–39, emphasis added)

Every act and word of Christ during His earthly life is significant. While we can't conclude just from this that the latter rain will fall on the last day of Tabernacles, it's something to consider. John applied Jesus' statement above to Pentecost, and that is a partial fulfillment, but the complete fulfillment, I believe, will be here, though it could possibly start at the beginning of the feast on the first day and build to the seventh.

Two other reasons for favoring Tabernacles are 1) the Day of Atonement, five days before, has removed the sins of spiritual Israel, as in the vision of Joshua and the Angel, and in that vision, the next scene is the oil of the Spirit being poured out from the two anointed ones to the seven lamps; and 2) Scripture says Tabernacles was the feast of the greatest rejoicing in Israel. When the latter rain is given, we will not only be grateful beyond words for our atonement but also filled with the Spirit of love and joy. We'll have peace like a river and joy like a fountain! Who can make us sad when Jesus makes us glad?

> *Scripture says Tabernacles was the feast of the greatest rejoicing in Israel. When the latter rain is given, we will not only be grateful beyond words for our atonement but also filled with the Spirit of love and joy. We'll have peace like a river and joy like a fountain! Who can make us sad when Jesus makes us glad?*

With that said, we ought to also watch for the fulfillment of prophetic events in the spring because, as we've seen, 1) the Feast of Unleavened

Bread has a future application, and 2) the week of atonement of Ezekiel's temple is still future—in the spring.

In the end times, the saints become aware, as that day approaches, that the time has come to earnestly petition God for the outpouring of His Spirit. Their strong intercessions come up before God with the fragrant incense of Christ's righteousness. The Father answers their prayers affirmatively, sending the fire of His Spirit on the waiting church (see Rev. 8:1–5). Immediately after this, the trumpets sound in quick succession.

Some will think this is futurism and date-setting, but if it is, all Jews are date-setters because they do this every year as well. Modern Judaism has this delightful Passover custom: At the start of the festive meal, a member of the household, usually a child, leaves the table, goes to the door of the home, and opens it to welcome Elijah. If Elijah is not there, then the family looks forward to welcoming him the following year. The Jews have done this for hundreds, perhaps thousands, of years.

Considering these things, is the Lord inviting us to pray for the refreshing especially at this feast? Given our propensity to put off spiritual preparation, I believe the Lord will give us signs, inviting and urging us to earnest prayer for His Spirit when the time comes.

At the early rain, the hearts of the disciples had been prepared for it by events that had shaken their faith to the core, especially the death of Christ. The crucifixion had fully exposed their human weakness, and they were now humble, joyful, and loving. Similarly, shortly before the latter rain, we can expect equally unnerving events that will humble us and put us in a prayerful, grateful frame of mind.

On the day of His ascension, Christ gathered His disciples and instructed them to wait in Jerusalem for the outpouring of His spirit (see Acts 1:1–9). During the following ten days, the disciples united in repentance, prayer, and especially praise as they looked for the fulfillment of the promise of the Comforter. On the tenth day, Pentecost, the Spirit came upon them in power. Similarly, we should prepare ourselves for that special time.

If nothing monumental happens this year, we shouldn't lose heart. The Lord hears every sincere prayer and is more willing to give the Holy Spirit to us than an earthly father is to give good gifts to his children. Regardless of what happens, let's not be asleep at the wheel. Let's be wiser than the wise virgins, having oil in reserve **and** remaining wide awake with our lamps trimmed and burning, ready to light the Bridegroom's way to the wedding.

Chapter 27

The Final Victory

Adventists have historically taught that the seventy weeks of Daniel 9 ended in AD 34, three-and-a-half years after the crucifixion. However, most are not aware that the final, end-time assault on the church through the abomination of desolation *and* the final victory of God's people are both also prophesied:

> Seventy weeks are determined upon thy people and upon thy holy city, *to finish the transgression, and to make an end of sins, and to make reconciliation for iniquity, and to bring in everlasting righteousness, and to seal up the vision and prophecy, and to anoint the most Holy.*... And he shall confirm the covenant with many for one week: and in the midst of the week he shall cause the sacrifice and the oblation to cease, and *for the overspreading of abominations he shall make it desolate, even until the consummation, and that determined shall be poured upon the desolate.* (Daniel 9:24, 27, emphasis added)

Referring to the final seven years of the 490-year period, it says, "He shall confirm the covenant with many for one week [seven years]." The final week, or seven years, of Daniel 9 began at the baptism of Christ in AD 27. From the time the Savior entered His ministry, the gospel was preached especially to the Jews: for three-and-a-half years by Christ Himself and another three-and-a-half years by the apostles. In the middle of that week, AD 31, Christ was crucified.

All these events confirm the fulfillment of the prophecy, except two important parts: 1) The "decreed end" was not "poured out on the desolator"; and 2) everlasting righteousness in the Israel of God was not established by the final atonement of Christ.

Notice how Daniel 9:27 reads in the ESV: "And he shall make a strong covenant with many for one week, and for half of the week he shall put an end to sacrifice and offering. And on the wing of abominations shall come one who makes desolate, until the decreed end is poured out on the desolator." The "wing of abominations" denotes a rapid persecuting onslaught, which is inflicted by the two beasts (see Rev. 13). This is the end-time abomination of desolation that Christ admonished us to study and understand so we will recognize and flee from it when we see it. These beasts are forming rapidly now in front of our eyes, but they have not fully "compassed [spiritual] Jerusalem" yet.

Equally significant, the establishment of everlasting righteousness in the church did not occur as foretold by the prophecy in AD 34. The Jews rejected their Messiah, and this was followed by the falling away of the church. As prophesied by the apostles, the church also apostatized. However, in the future, when Daniel 9 is fulfilled, everlasting righteousness will be eternally secured; at the close of the 2,300 days, the "sons of Levi" will be cleansed; sin and transgression in Zion and Israel will end (see verse 24). Isaiah, like Daniel, also prophesied this:

> And it shall come to pass, that he that is left in Zion, and he that remaineth in Jerusalem, shall be called holy, even every one that is written among the living in Jerusalem: When the Lord shall have washed away the filth of the daughters of Zion, and shall have purged the blood of Jerusalem from the midst thereof by the spirit of judgment, and by the spirit of burning. And the LORD will create upon every dwelling place of mount Zion, and upon her assemblies, a cloud and smoke by day, and the shining of a flaming fire by night: for upon all the glory shall be a defense. And there shall be a tabernacle for a shadow in the daytime from the heat, and for a place of refuge, and for a covert from storm and from rain. (Isaiah 4:3–6)

This is a further description of the final atonement of Christ when the sanctuary is cleansed at the close of the 2,300 days, and that is good news. It was the hope of all the prophets and apostles. The liberation of the Israel of God and her purification from sin results in the establishment of His kingdom and the everlasting covenant, which is the central hope of the saints. The prayer Christ taught us to pray will be answered: "Thy kingdom come, thy will be done on earth as it is in heaven" (Matt. 6:10). His kingdom will be established in our hearts and souls.

The Cleansing of the 2,300 Days

> Then I heard one saint speaking, and another saint said unto that certain saint which spake, How long shall be the vision concerning the daily sacrifice, and the transgression of desolation, to give both the sanctuary and the host to be trodden under foot? And he said unto me, Unto two thousand and three hundred days; then shall the sanctuary be cleansed. (Daniel 8:13, 14)

The above passage, more than any other, was the inspiration for the second great awakening of the early nineteenth century, pointing God's people to the work of Christ in their final cleansing.

Unfortunately, while the early Adventists understood God was about to do a great work on earth, they didn't make the direct application to themselves that He intended. Their faith, like ours, needed to grow and expand until they made that essential, direct, personal application—"The final atonement of Christ is personally for me."

In earlier manuscripts of this book, I set out arguments that from a literal reading of Daniel 8 and 9, both of these prophecies meet their complete fulfillment in our day.[14] Both take us to just before the return of Christ, when He completes His atonement and presents His bride to Himself, robed in the wedding gown of His dazzling white righteousness.

> *Unfortunately, while the early Adventists understood God was about to do a great work on earth, they didn't make the direct application to themselves that He intended. Their faith, like ours, needed to grow and expand until they made that essential, direct, personal application — "The final atonement of Christ is personally for me."*

However, I've removed those chapters from this edition. Why? Because I want to underline the point that the key element is faith. Like Israel in the wilderness, none of us will enter the Promised Land, however clear the prophecies may be, without faith. If we do have it, then we'll simply take God at His word that "sin shall not have dominion over you" (Rom. 6:14) and, like Abraham, our belief will be reckoned to us for righteousness (see 4:3).

---

[14] I don't plan at this time to publish these chapters, but if readers would like a copy for their study, please email me at Mark.Shipowick@gmail.com.

The Word advises us, therefore, to take inventory of our faith because without it, it is impossible to please God (see Heb. 11:6). Without a living, working faith, the final atonement of Christ for us will be fruitless. By contrast, if we have the genuine article and learn to consistently exercise and nurture it, becoming strong in the Lord and the power of His might, we will be established on the Rock, immovable, children of God, and heirs of the glorious inheritance of the saints in light.

> Cast not away therefore your confidence, which hath great recompence of reward. For ye have need of patience, that, after ye have done the will of God, ye might receive the promise. For yet a little while, and he that shall come will come, and will not tarry. Now the just shall live by faith: but if any man draw back, my soul shall have no pleasure in him. But we are not of them who draw back unto perdition; but of them that believe to the saving of the soul. (Hebrews 10:35–39)

Appendix A

The Sanctuary Doctrine by J. N. Andrews

One of the foremost nineteenth-century expositors of the sanctuary was John N. Andrews. The following twelve paragraphs are a condensed excerpt from his article "The Sanctuary" in the October 22, 1874, issue of *The Signs of the Times*:

The Bible doctrine of the sanctuary is this: That the sanctuary is the place where the High Priest stands to offer blood before God for the sins of those who come to God through him. The central object in the sanctuary is the ark which contains the law of God that man has broken. The cover of this ark was called the mercy-seat, because mercy came to those who had broken the law beneath it, when the High priest sprinkled the blood of sin-offering upon it, provided he accompanied his work by repentance and faith. Last of all was the work of cleansing the sanctuary when the high priest by blood removed the sins of the people from the sanctuary into which they had been borne by the ministration of the priests before God. We now invite attention to the testimony of the Bible respecting the sanctuary.

1. There are two covenants; the first, or old covenant, extends from the time of Moses to the death of Christ; the second, or new covenant, begins at the death of Christ and extends forward to the consummation. Gal. 4:24–26; Heb. 8:7–13; Luke 22:20.
2. The first covenant had a sanctuary, which was the tabernacle erected by Moses. Heb. 9:1–17.

3. The new covenant has a sanctuary which is the temple of God in Heaven, into which our High Priest entered when he ascended upon high. Heb. 8:1–5.
4. When Moses erected the tabernacle, he was commanded by God to make it according to the pattern which he showed to him; and this pattern must have been a representation of the temple of God in Heaven; for the earthly sanctuary is declared to be a pattern of the heavenly. Ex. 25:9, 40; Heb. 8:5; 9:23....

The word sanctuary in the Bible, except in the few cases where it is used figuratively, refers always to the place in which the high priests ministers before God for the sins of the people. It was first the tabernacle erected by Moses; then it was the temple built by Solomon, which was a more glorious structure than the tabernacle, but with the same two holy places; and when the typical sacrifices ended in the death of Christ, who is the true sin offering, the earthly sanctuary, or, holy 'places', ceased to be the center of God's worship, and Christ entered the temple in Heaven as a great High Priest—"the minister of the sanctuary and of the true tabernacle, which the Lord, pitched, and not man." Heb 8:2. The temple of God in Heaven is the sanctuary from which the psalmist says the Lord beheld the earth (Ps. 102:19), and which Jeremiah speaks of as being where the throne of God is found. Jer. 17:12; Rev. 16:17.

The ministration in the earthly sanctuary could not actually take away sins; for it had only the blood of bulls and goats to offer. Heb. 10:4. It was given to Israel for the purpose of instructing them with reference to the work of Christ, and of encouraging them to look forward to his work. It is a shadow or representation of the service of Christ in the sanctuary of God in Heaven. Heb. 8:5; 10: 1; Col. 2:17. It took one year to complete the round of service in the earthly sanctuary, at the end of which the cleansing of the sanctuary took place. The round of service was repeated each year, even as a shadow is renewed each day. But the ministration of Christ which casts this shadow fills out each part of the work once for all, and is not repeated....

It is certain, therefore, that just as there was a time each year devoted to the finishing up of the round of service in "the example and shadow of heavenly things" so there is also such a period in the conclusion of Christ's ministration, when once for all our High Priest finishes his work of priesthood; and as this work in the former dispensation took place in the second apartment, so also under the New Covenant does this work find its accomplishment within the second veil by the ark of the ten commandments....

The work within the second apartment was for the cleansing of the sanctuary, and this was performed by the high priest with blood, and when it was accomplished the sins of the people were blotted out. It was, therefore, an event of the greatest importance to the people of God. The heavenly sanctuary is to be cleansed, and for the same reason that the earthly sanctuary was cleansed. So Paul testifies in Heb. 9:23.... The prophecy of Daniel 8:14 shows us that the sanctuary of God is cleansed in the last days of the New Covenant dispensation. The time marked for its cleansing is that fixed by John for the opening of the temple in Heaven and for the finishing of the mystery of God. Rev. 11:19; 10:7....

[T]he object of this final work in the sanctuary is to determine who are worthy of everlasting life... The investigation will determine who have overcome their sins; and these will have their sins blotted from the record, and their names retained in the book of life. It will also determine who have not overcome and these will have their names blotted from the book of life, Rev. 3:5, and their sins will be retained in the record, to be visited with retribution in the resurrection to damnation....

The righteous need a high priest until .their sins are blotted out. They cannot be blotted out till the Judgment; for God has decreed to bring every work into judgment whether good or evil. Eccl. 12:13, 14; 3:17. He certainly cannot bring any record into judgment after he has blotted it out. The blotting out is therefore the last act of our High Priest, and is done when the Father has accounted each person worthy of this; which will only be when the High Priest has shown from the record in the book of God's remembrance that he has actually overcome. The blotting out of sins (Acts 3:19) is therefore the great work which brings our Lord's priesthood to a conclusion. As this is an individual work, it evidently begins with the first generation of the righteous, and so comes down to the last, that is, to those who are alive at the coming of Christ. It is the time of the dead that they should be judged. Rev. 11:18, 19. The first angel gives notice to the inhabitants of the earth that the hour of God's judgment has come. Rev. 14:6, 7. The living are still on probation when this solemn announcement is made to mankind.

The proclamation of the third angel, which is made while Christ is closing up his work in the sanctuary is designed to prepare the living for the decision of the Judgment. When the cases of the living are reached, [and fully judged] probation closes up forever. The decree goes forth from the throne of God, "He that is unjust, let him be unjust still and lie that is holy, let him be holy still." Rev. 22:11.

The sins of the overcomers being blotted out, and the sanctuary cleansed, the Son of God is no longer needed as a great High Priest. He therefore ceases from the office forever and becomes a king for the deliverance and glorification of his people, and for the destruction of all transgressors. Dan. 7:13, 14. Satan, the author of sin, receives its dreadful burden when the work in the sanctuary is closed, and will bear it with him to the lake of fire.

It is of infinite consequence to us who live in the time when Christ is closing up his priesthood, that we understand the work which he is performing, and that we so walk in the light as to share in his great salvation. J. N. ANDREWS.

Appendix B

Time-Setting Statements by Ellen White

Adventists have been inoculated from virtually all forms of date-setting by our early history and the inspired statements of Scripture and Ellen White. Unfortunately, while these texts are accurate and balanced, we have been over-vaccinated by modern expositors who read more into them than they ought, with the result being that end-time prophecies are being quenched in our day, especially by the conservative segment of the church.

Christ is specific about what has not been revealed. His parting instruction to the apostles after His resurrection was, "It is not for you to know the times or the seasons, which the Father hath put in his own power" (Acts 1:7). Two thousand years later, His instruction still applies. However, we should remember that on the same occasion and virtually in the same breath, the Lord also promised to bestow on the church the gift of the Holy Spirit, which is especially demonstrated in the prophetic gift. That gift is irrevocable and remains in effect in the church to the close of time (see 1 Cor. 14; Rom. 11:29).

> "Adventists have been inoculated from virtually all forms of date-setting by our early history and the inspired statements of Scripture and Ellen White. Unfortunately, while these texts are accurate and balanced, we have been over-vaccinated by modern expositors who read more into them than they ought, with the result being that end-time prophecies are being quenched in our day, especially by the conservative segment of the church."

That there are time prophecies after 1844 is clear from Daniel 12 and Revelation's seven seals, trumpets, the periods in chapters 11–13, and the millennium. Adventists are largely unprepared for their fulfillment because for most of our history, we've been in denial of their future application. And the reason for this is our over-vaccination. Notwithstanding clear statements by Ellen White regarding their future application, these prophecies have been relegated to the past because of their time elements. These deserve our careful re-examination. They are central to the warning of Christ to study and understand the abomination of desolation, an issue of gravity and consequence for the final generation.

At the dawn of Israel's history, Joseph told Pharaoh, king of the greatest, most advanced empire of that time (the pyramids are still regarded as a marvel of engineering), that seven years of plenty would be followed by seven years of famine. Through the prophetic gift, God saved not only the Egyptians but also the Israelites and much of the ancient world. That same gift will operate in the church to the close of time. Rather than quenching the Spirit, let's be grateful for the Lord's mercy to us. "Surely the Lord GOD will do nothing, but he revealeth his secret unto his servants the prophets" (Amos 3:7).

In keeping with Christ's instructions, no one is to preach definite dates for the outpouring of the Spirit or His return. However, we ought to expect the Lord will give the church insights into the many prophecies that are on the verge of fulfillment. These are not tests of faith. They are given to warn and comfort the church, which will see in them the unmistakable tokens of the Lord's soon return and, like Pharaoh and the Egyptians did under Joseph, govern themselves according to their warnings.

The inspired passages below are representative of the most comprehensive statements against time setting. They accurately expound the meaning of Christ's statement above:

> I plainly stated at the Jackson camp meeting to these fanatical parties that they were doing the work of the adversary of souls; they were in darkness. They claimed to have great light that probation would close in October, 1884. I there stated in public that the Lord had been pleased to show me that there would be no definite time in the message given of God since 1844....
>
> Our position has been one of waiting and watching, with no time-proclamation to intervene between the close of the prophetic periods in 1844 and the time of our Lord's coming....

The people will not have another message upon definite time. After this period of time [Revelation 10:4–6], reaching from 1842 to 1844, there can be no definite tracing of the prophetic time. The longest reckoning reaches to the autumn of 1844. (White, *Last Day Events*, pp. 35, 36)

I have borne the testimony since the passing of the time in 1844, that there should be no definite time set by which to test God's people. The great test on time was in 1843 and 1844; and all who have set time since these great periods marked in prophecy were deceiving and being deceived. (White, *Life Sketches of James White and Ellen G. White 1880*, pp. 221, 222)

Let all our brethren and sisters beware of anyone who would set a time for the Lord to fulfill His word in regard to His coming, or in regard to any other promise He has made of special significance. (White, *Testimonies to Ministers and Gospel Workers*, p. 55)

Appendix C

The Dark Day and Falling of the Stars

Adventists apply the prophecies of the darkening of the sun, the moon turning to blood, and the falling of the stars (see Joel 2, 3; Rev. 6) to certain remarkable events in the eighteenth and nineteenth centuries. While these prophecies also have a future application, it is helpful to review their initial fulfillment to gain a clearer view of how they may be fulfilled again. While the past gives us some indication, we should also realize the future fulfillments could well be even more extensive and dramatic.

"In the morning the sun rose clear, but was soon overcast. The clouds became lower, and from them, black and ominous, as they soon appeared, lightning flashed, thunder rolled, and a little rain fell. Toward nine o'clock, the clouds became thinner, and assumed a brassy or coppery appearance, and earth, rocks, trees, buildings, water, and persons were changed by this strange, unearthly light. A few minutes later, a heavy black cloud spread over the entire sky except a narrow rim at the horizon, and it was as dark as it usually is at nine o'clock on a summer evening....

"Fear, anxiety, and awe gradually filled the minds of the people. Women stood at the door, looking out upon the dark landscape; men returned from their labor in the fields; the carpenter left his tools, the blacksmith his forge, the tradesman his counter. Schools were dismissed, and tremblingly the children fled homeward. Travelers put up at the nearest farmhouse. 'What is coming?' queried every lip and heart. It seemed as if a hurricane was about to dash across the land, or as if it was the day of the consummation of all things.

"Candles were used; and hearth fires shone as brightly as on a moonless evening in autumn.... Fowls retired to their roosts and went to sleep, cattle gathered at the pasture bars and lowed, frogs peeped, birds sang their evening songs, and bats flew about. But the human knew that night had not come....

"Dr. Nathanael Whittaker, pastor of the Tabernacle church in Salem, held religious services in the meeting-house, and preached a sermon in which he maintained that the darkness was supernatural. Congregations came together in many other places. The texts for the extemporaneous sermons were invariably those that seemed to indicate that the darkness was consonant with Scriptural prophecy.... The darkness was most dense shortly after eleven o'clock."... "In most parts of the country it was so great in the daytime, that the people could not tell the hour by either watch or clock, nor dine, nor manage their domestic business, without the light of candles....

"The extent of this darkness was extraordinary. It was observed as far east as Falmouth. To the westward it reached to the farthest part of Connecticut, and to Albany. To the southward, it was observed along the seacoasts; and to the north as far as the American settlements extend."...

The intense darkness of the day was succeeded, an hour or two before evening, by a partially clear sky, and the sun appeared, though it was still obscured by the black, heavy mist. "After sundown, the clouds came again overhead, and it grew dark very fast." "Nor was the darkness of the night less uncommon and terrifying than that of the day; notwithstanding there was almost a full moon, no object was discernible but by the help of some artificial light, which, when seen from the neighboring houses and other places at a distance, appeared through a kind of Egyptian darkness which seemed almost impervious to the rays."... Said an eyewitness of the scene: "I could not help conceiving at the time, that if every luminous body in the universe had been shrouded in impenetrable shades, or struck out of existence, the darkness could not have been more complete."... Though at nine o'clock that night the moon rose to the full, "it had not the least effect to dispel the deathlike shadows." After midnight the darkness disappeared, and the moon, when first visible, had the appearance of blood.

May 19, 1780, stands in history as "The Dark Day." Since the time of Moses no period of darkness of equal density, extent, and duration, has ever been recorded. The description of this event, as given by eyewitnesses, is but an echo of the words of the Lord, recorded by the prophet Joel, twenty-five hundred years previous to their fulfillment: "The sun shall be turned into darkness, and the moon into blood, before the great and terrible day of the Lord come." (White, *The Great Controversy*, pp. 306–308)

The same source also documents the falling of the stars:

In 1833, two years after Miller began to present in public the evidences of Christ's soon coming, the last of the signs appeared which were promised by the Saviour as tokens of His second advent. Said Jesus: "The stars shall fall from heaven." Matthew 24:29. And John in the Revelation declared, as he beheld in vision the scenes that should herald the day of God: "The stars of heaven fell unto the earth, even as a fig tree casteth her untimely figs, when she is shaken of a mighty wind." Revelation 6:13. This prophecy received a striking and impressive fulfillment in the great meteoric shower of November 13, 1833. That was the most extensive and wonderful display of falling stars which has ever been recorded; "the whole firmament, over all the United States, being then, for hours, in fiery commotion! No celestial phenomenon has ever occurred in this country, since its first settlement, which was viewed with such intense admiration by one class in the community, or with so much dread and alarm by another." "Its sublimity and awful beauty still linger in many minds.... Never did rain fall much thicker than the meteors fell toward the earth; east, west, north, and south, it was the same. In a word, the whole heavens seemed in motion. The display, as described in Professor Silliman's *Journal*, was seen all over North America.... From two o'clock until broad daylight, the sky being perfectly serene and cloudless, an incessant play of dazzlingly brilliant luminosities was kept up in the whole heavens."...

"No language, indeed, can come up to the splendor of that magnificent display; ... no one who did not witness it can form an adequate conception of its glory. It seemed as if the whole starry heavens had congregated at one point near the zenith, and were simultaneously shooting forth, with the velocity of lightning, to every part of the horizon; and yet they were not exhausted—thousands swiftly followed in the tracks of thousands, as if created for the occasion.".... "A more correct picture of a fig tree casting its figs when blown by a mighty wind, it was not possible to behold."...

In the New York *Journal of Commerce* of November 14, 1833, appeared a long article regarding this wonderful phenomenon, containing this statement: "No philosopher or scholar has told or recorded an event, I suppose, like that of yesterday morning. A prophet eighteen hundred years ago foretold it exactly, if we will be at the trouble of understanding stars falling to mean falling stars, ... in the only sense in which it is possible to be literally true."

Thus was displayed the last of those signs of His coming, concerning which Jesus bade His disciples: "When ye shall see all these things, *know* that it is near, even at the doors." Matthew 24:33. After these signs, John beheld, as the great event next impending, the heavens departing as a scroll, while the earth quaked, mountains and islands removed out of their places, and the wicked in terror sought to flee from the presence of the Son of man. Revelation 6:12–17.

Many who witnessed the falling of the stars, looked upon it as a herald of the coming judgment, "an awful type, a sure forerunner, a merciful sign, of that great and dreadful day."... Thus the attention of the people was directed to the fulfillment of prophecy, and many were led to give heed to the warning of the second advent. (White, *The Great Controversy*, pp. 333, 334)

Appendix D

Thutmose III and the Lateran Connection

The Lateran Treaty of 1929 is of interest to Christians, as it marks a significant milestone in the healing of the head wound of the beast at the end of the 1,260 years of papal supremacy. Pius VI was taken hostage by Napoleon's General Berthier in 1798 and died in exile in France the next year. Two years later, the papal states were restored to the papacy by the French Consulate until 1809, when they were annexed to the French Empire and then restored again to the papacy in 1814. They remained under papal control until the early 1860s, when they became a part of Italy. Following this humiliation, the papacy was reduced to the status of a religious office and enjoyed no political prominence as a head of state—until 1929.

Many Christians are not aware that before the papacy's humiliation by Napoleon, the popes of the Dark Ages lived lavishly in the Lateran Palace and governed Christendom from this basilica for a millennium: from the fourth century until the fourteenth century. Beginning in the early 1300s, the popes lived in other locations, eventually residing in their current location in the Vatican Palace. However, it is noteworthy that by long tradition, although the popes have occupied other palaces, the Lateran Basilica has retained its primacy as Archbasilica, seat of the pontiff, and its status as the mother church.

Thus, in 1929, when the wound was partially healed, the Lateran Treaty was signed in the Lateran Palace, and Benito Mussolini, the Italian head of state, reinstated the rights of the pope as head of state, not only of the Vatican, but also the Archbasilica of Lateran itself and other real estate enclaves in Rome and Italy as "extraterritorial property."

Many are under the impression that the Vatican is the seat of the papacy, but in fact, this is not the case. The archbasilica (meaning "greatest basilica"), which holds the papal throne, is, in fact, not St. Peter's Basilica in the Vatican, but the Lateran Basilica, which, unlike the Vatican, is within the ancient walls of the seven-hilled City of Rome.

Regarding the *cathedra* ("papal throne"), the throne and title of the Caesars was transferred to the pope in AD 538, and he became the *Pontifex Maximus* ("highest or chief priest"). This title was held by the pagan emperors of Rome before the popes, beginning with Caesar Augustus and including Tiberius Caesar in the time of Christ.

Thus, the apocalyptic prophecy was and is fulfilled: "The dragon gave him his power, and his **seat**, and great authority" (Rev. 13:2). It is noteworthy that this prophecy actually does have a quite literal fulfillment in the Lateran Archbasilica, where the papal throne resides:

Figure 8: Lateran Archbasilica

In the sixth century the papacy had become firmly established. Its *seat* of power was fixed in the imperial city, and the bishop of Rome was declared to be the head over the entire church. Paganism had given place to the papacy. The dragon had given to the beast "his power, and his seat, and great authority." Revelation 13:2. And now began the 1260 years of papal oppression foretold in the prophecies of Daniel and the Revelation. (White, *The Great Controversy*, p. 54, emphasis added)

With that background, what follows is a more detailed, fascinating history of the Lateran Basilica itself:

The church is the oldest and highest ranking of the four papal major basilicas ... holding the unique title of "archbasilica" ... it is the oldest public church in the city of Rome, and the oldest basilica of the Western world. It houses the *cathedra* [i.e., throne] of the Roman bishop, and has the title of ecumenical mother church of the Catholic faithful....

As the cathedral of the pope as bishop of Rome, it ranks superior to all other churches of the Catholic Church, including Saint Peter's Basilica....

The archbasilica is sited in the City of Rome. It is outside Vatican City, which is approximately 4 kilometers (2.5 mi) to its northwest, although the archbasilica and its adjoining edifices have extraterritorial status from Italy as one of the properties of the Holy See, pursuant to the Lateran Treaty of 1929.

The current rector is Cardinal Archpriest Angelo De Donatis, Vicar General *[of the pope]* for the Diocese of Rome. The President of the French Republic, currently Emmanuel Macron, is *ex officio* the "first and only honorary canon" of the archbasilica, a title that the heads of state of France have possessed since King Henry IV.

[Originally, the archbasilica was a palace belonging to an ancient and prominent Roman family bearing the Lateran name.] Their palace and property fell into the hands of the Emperor when Constantine I married his second wife Fausta, sister of Maxentius. *[Constantine was the first Christian Roman Emperor who is supposed to have converted to Christianity as the result of a vision during a military campaign and who, in 321 AD issued a decree to establish Sunday sacredness throughout the empire by honoring the Roman sun god to unite its pagan and Christian elements.]*

Known by that time as the "Domus Faustae" or "House of Fausta," the Lateran Palace was eventually given to the Bishop of Rome by

Constantine I. The actual date of the donation is unknown, but scholars speculate that it was during the pontificate of Pope Miltiades, in time to host a synod of bishops in 313 that was convened to challenge the Donatist schism, declaring Donatism to be heresy. The palace basilica was converted and extended, becoming the residence of Pope Sylvester I, eventually becoming the Cathedral of Rome, the seat of the Popes as the Bishops of Rome.

Pope Sylvester I presided over the official dedication of the archbasilica and the adjacent Lateran Palace in 324, changing the name from "Domus Fausta" to "Domus Dei" ("House of God") with a dedication to Christ the Savior ("Christo Salvatori"). When a cathedra, *[a papal throne]*, became a symbol of episcopal authority, the papal cathedra was placed in its interior, rendering it the cathedral of the Pope as Bishop of Rome.

When Gregory the Great sent the Gregorian mission to England under Augustine of Canterbury, some original churches in Canterbury took the Roman plan as a model, dedicating a church both to Christ as well as one to Saint Paul, outside the walls of the city. The church name "Christ Church", so common for churches around the world today in Anglophone Anglican contexts, originally came from this Roman church, central to pre-medieval Christian identity.

On the archbasilica's front wall between the main portals is a plaque inscribed with the words "SACROS LATERAN ECCLES OMNIUM VRBIS ET ORBIS ECCLESIARVM MATER ET CAPUT" "Most Holy Lateran Church, mother and head of all the churches in the city and the world"; a visible indication of the declaration that the basilica is the "mother church" of all the world. In the twelfth century the canons of the Lateran claimed that the high altar housed the Ark of the Covenant and several holy objects from Jerusalem. The basilica was thus presented as the Temple of the New Covenant.

Every pope, beginning with Pope Miltiades, occupied the Lateran Palace until the reign of the French Pope Clement V, who in 1309 transferred the seat of the Papacy to Avignon, a Papal fiefdom that was an enclave in France. The Lateran Palace has also been the site of five ecumenical councils.

During the time the papacy was seated in Avignon, France, the Lateran Palace and the archbasilica deteriorated. Two fires ravaged them in 1307 and 1361. When the papacy returned from Avignon and the pope again resided in Rome, the archbasilica and the Lateran Palace were deemed inadequate considering their accumulated damage.

There were several attempts at reconstruction of the archbasilica before a definitive program of Pope Sixtus V. Sixtus V hired his favorite architect, Domenico Fontana, to supervise much of the project. The original Lateran Palace was demolished and replaced with a new edifice. On the square in front of the Lateran Palace is the largest standing obelisk in the world, known as the Lateran Obelisk. It weighs an estimated 455 tons. It was commissioned by the Egyptian Pharaoh Thutmose III and erected by Thutmose IV before the great Karnak temple of Thebes, Egypt. Intended by Emperor Constantine I to be shipped to Constantinople, the very preoccupied Constantius II had it shipped instead to Rome, where it was erected in the Circus Maximus in AD 357. At some time it broke and was buried under the Circus. In the 16th century it was discovered and excavated, and Sixtus V had it re-erected on a new pedestal on 3 August 1588 at its present site. [*End of article but notice the date the obelisk was re- erected, 1588.*][15]

The Obelisk of Thutmose III and the Throne

According to scholars who hold to the high view of Egyptian chronology, Thutmose III, the Pharaoh who commissioned the obelisk, reigned from 1504–1450 BC. This monarch is possibly the Pharaoh of the Exodus based on Bible chronology. Egyptian records corroborate this, indicating that his firstborn son predeceased him—likely slain by the destroying angel at the first Passover—and the throne of Egypt would have passed down, upon the father's drowning in the Red Sea, to his second eldest, Thutmose IV.

Ancient Egyptian records state that this son completed the obelisk to honor his father and the Egyptian sun god Ra and erected it at the great Karnak Temple of Thebes. It stood there for seventeen centuries until Constantine I (the emperor who also defied heaven, venerating the same pagan sun god, *Sol Invictus*, to the Romans and established Sunday sacredness throughout the empire in AD 321 AD) sought to bring it to Constantinople, the new seat of the Eastern Empire. However, as stated above, after Constantine's death, instead, his son had it erected on the *spina*, the middle barrier of the Circus Maximus of Rome, venue for the ever popular Roman chariot races.

Amazingly, but perhaps not surprisingly, today this 3,400-year-old monolith stands by the mother church of Rome on its northwest side,

---

[15] "Archbasilica of Saint John Lateran," Wikimedia Foundation, last modified May 16, 2023, https://en.wikipedia.org/wiki/Archbasilica_of_Saint_John_Lateran.

topped with a cross but still venerating the sun as Pharaoh intended, gracing the front yard of the palace of the archbasilica, where the cathedra seat of the pope resides today as it did throughout the Dark Ages.

This seat takes its inspiration from the mercy seat over the ark of the covenant in the Most Holy Place. Here, in the westernmost part of the nave, like in the ancient Hebrew temple, it is placed with pomp and symbol on a raised platform in the center of the apse, the most holy place of the archbasilica at its western focus, still the place of enthronement for the pontiffs—a donation of Constantine.[16]

Figure 9: Obelisk of Thutmose III in front of the Lateran Palace

---

[16] The ancient documents that donated the Lateran Palace and conferred authority over the western Roman Empire on the pope is one of the largest deceptions known to western civilization. The Donation of Constantine was included in the ninth-century Pseudo-Isidorian decretals, all of which were conclusively shown to be forgeries in the fifteenth and following centuries (see https://en.wikipedia.org/wiki/Donation_of_Constantine).

Appendix E

153 and 666

The numbers 153 and 666, both found in Scripture, are two of the most interesting and "symmetrical" numbers in mathematics. Their properties are summarized below.

Regarding 153, just before His crucifixion, Jesus told His disciples to meet Him in Galilee after His resurrection. Following His direction, they gathered there waiting, but when night fell and Christ hadn't come, Peter, wanting to be productive, said, "I'm going fishing." Peter, James, and John, all of them skilled fishermen, caught nothing that night, but as dawn was breaking, Christ called to them from the shore, asking them if they had caught anything. They told Him "no," and then He told them to let down their nets again, but on the other side of the boat. When they did, their net immediately filled with so many large fish that it was in danger of braking yet didn't. When they counted the catch, there were 153 large, healthy fish.

The number 153 has several mathematical properties making it perhaps the most "symmetrical" number. It is the sum of the first 17 integers (i.e., $1 + 2 + 3 + ... + 16 + 17 = 153$); it is also the sum of the first five positive factorials (i.e., $1! + 2! + 3! + 4! + 5!$). The number 153 is associated with the geometric shape known as the *vesica piscis* ("bladder of a fish"), formed by the intersection of two circles of the same radius at their centers creating a lens. Archimedes, an ancient Greek mathematician, in his *Measurement of a Circle*, referred to the width-to-height ratio of this lens as 153/265, constituting the "measure of the fish," this ratio being an imperfect representation of $1/\sqrt{3}$, which is approximately 0.577350269189 62576450914878050196.

The number 153 is both a triangular number and a hexagonal number, meaning 153 symmetrical objects such as spheres will form an equilateral

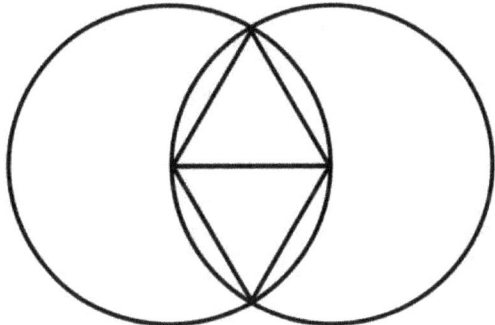

triangle or hexagon when evenly spaced in rows. It is also a truncated triangle number, meaning 1, 15, and 153 are all triangular numbers.

The number 153 is the smallest three-digit number that can be expressed as the sum of cubes of its digits. Only three other numbers can be expressed as the sum of the cubes of their digits: 370, 371, and 407. It is also a Friedman number, since 153 = 3 x 51, and a Harshad number in base 10, being divisible by the sum of its own digits.[17]

In base 36, 153 is 49, which is 7 x 7 in base 10—double perfection or completion. Compare this with 666, which in base 36 is II—that is, the double letter I as in "me, me."

Finally, as noted in the text, another remarkable feature of the number 153 is that it is the limit of the following algorithm:

1. Take any random positive integer divisible by three.
2. Split that number into its base 10 digits.
3. Take the sum of their cubes.
4. Repeat steps 2 and 3, and eventually the number will be 153.

Additionally, since $1^3 \times 5^3 \times 3^3$ = 153, this is the limit of all integers divisible by 3 whose digits are separated, cubed, and summed. Therefore, 153 is a fit symbol of the limit and the sum of the final harvest of the righteous.

The number 666 has a kind of symmetry as well. Like 153, which is the sum of the first 17 natural numbers, 666 is the sum of the first 36 natural numbers (i.e., 1 + 2 + 3 + ... + 34 + 35 + 36 = 666) and thus also a triangular number, like 153 is, but not a hexagonal number. It is also *not* the sum of the first six positive factorials, as 153 is of the first five. However, 666 *is*

---

[17] See "153 (number)," Wikipedia Foundation, last modified June 4, 2023, https://en.wikipedia.org/wiki/153_(number)

the sum of the squares of the first seven prime numbers (i.e., $2^2 + 3^2 + 5^2 + 7^2 + 11^2 + 13^2 + 17^2 = 666$). Now notice this series does not start with 1 but instead with 2 because according to academia, 2 is the first prime number (Modern mathematicians define a prime number as any natural number that has only two divisors: itself and 1. Since 1 has only one divisor, it doesn't fit the definition. What mathematicians overlook is that numbers are like words: They are symbols of the created reality deriving their meaning from the Creator. "Prime" in English means "first and foremost." To exclude 1 from the definition of prime numbers by creating a limited human definition is to ignore both the common meaning of the word and the reality, which is that God, who is one, is Prime).

The prime factorization of 666 is $2 \times 3^2 \times 37$. Compare this with the prime factorization of 153, which is $3^2 \times 17$.

The Roman numeral for 666, DCLXVI, has exactly one occurrence of every symbol whose value is under 1,000, in decreasing order (D = 500, C = 100, L = 50, X = 10, V = 5, I = 1).

The fourth and final beast of Daniel 7 that has ten horns is the same beast in Revelation 13 and 17 that has seven heads and ten horns—Rome in its three phases: pagan, papal, and revived, neo-pagan/papal.

The invitation of Christ is to be among the gospel harvest, symbolized by the 153 fish, and not among those who are numbered with the beast and its image who will be cast alive with them into the lake of fire (see Rev. 13:18; 14:9–12).

****

The Spirit and the Bride say, Come. And let him that heareth say, Come. And let him that is athirst come. And whosoever will, let him take The water of life freely.

Revelation 22:17

Bibliography

White, Ellen G. *Christ's Object Lessons.* Washington, DC: Review and Herald Publishing Association, 1900.

———. *Early Writings.* Washington, DC: Review and Herald Publishing Association, 1882.

———. *The Great Controversy.* Mountain View, CA: Pacific Press Publishing Association, 1911.

———. *The Kress Collection.* Payson, AZ: Leaves-of-Autumn Books, 1985.

———. *Last Day Events.* Boise, ID: Pacific Press Publishing Association, 1992.

———. *Letters and Manuscripts.* Vol. 16. Silver Spring, MD: Ellen G. White Estate, 1901.

———. *Life Sketches of Ellen G. White.* Mountain View, CA: Pacific Press Publishing Association, 1915.

———. *Life Sketches of James White and Ellen G. White 1880.* Battle Creek, MI: Seventh-day Adventist Publishing Association, 1880.

———. *Manuscript Releases.* Vol. 10. Silver Spring, MD: Ellen G. White Estate, 1990.

———. *Manuscript Releases.* Vol. 11. Silver Spring, MD: Ellen G. White Estate, 1990.

———. *Manuscript Releases.* Vol. 13. Silver Spring, MD: Ellen G. White Estate, 1990.

———. *Manuscript Releases.* Vol. 14. Silver Spring, MD: Ellen G. White Estate, 1990.

———. *Manuscript Releases.* Vol. 15. Silver Spring, MD: Ellen G. White Estate, 1990.

———. *Manuscript Releases.* Vol. 17. Silver Spring, MD: Ellen G. White Estate, 1990.

———. *Manuscript Releases.* Vol. 19. Silver Spring, MD: Ellen G. White Estate, 1990.

———. *Manuscript Releases.* Vol. 20. Silver Spring, MD: Ellen G. White Estate, 1993.

———. *Manuscript Releases.* Vol. 21. Silver Spring, MD: Ellen G. White Estate, 1993.

———. *Maranatha.* Washington, DC: Review and Herald Publishing Association, 1976.

———. *Our High Calling.* Washington, DC: Review and Herald Publishing Association, 1961.

———. "Pray for the Latter Rain," *The Review and Herald,* March 2, 1897.

———. *The SDA Bible Commentary.* Vol. 7. Washington, DC: Review and Herald Publishing Association, 1957.

———. *Selected Messages.* Book 1. Washington, DC: Review and Herald Publishing Association, 1958.

———. *Selected Messages.* Book 3. Washington, DC: Review and Herald Publishing Association, 1980.

———. *Testimonies for the Church.* Vol. 1. Mountain View, CA: Pacific Press Publishing Association, 1868.

———. *Testimonies for the Church.* Vol. 5. Mountain View, CA: Pacific Press Publishing Association, 1889.

———. *Testimonies for the Church.* Vol. 8. Mountain View, CA: Pacific Press Publishing Association, 1904.

———. *Testimonies for the Church.* Vol. 9. Mountain View, CA: Pacific Press Publishing Association, 1909.

———. *Testimonies to Ministers and Gospel Workers.* Mountain View, CA: Pacific Press Publishing Association, 1923.

———. *That I May Know Him.* Washington, DC: Review and Herald Publishing Association, 1964.

———. "What Shall We Do That We Might Work the Works of God?" *The Review and Herald,* April 21, 1891.

———. *A Word to the Little Flock.* Washington, DC: Review and Herald Publishing Association, 1847.

Endnotes

i   Adventists have taught that when Michael stands up, probation closes for everyone, but Ellen White addressed the peril of believers at that time:

> Oh, that the people might know the time of their visitation! There are many who have not yet heard the testing truth for this time. There are many with whom the Spirit of God is striving. The time of God's destructive judgments is the time of mercy for those who have had no opportunity to learn what is truth. Tenderly will the Lord look upon them. His heart of mercy is touched; His hand is still stretched out to save, while the door is closed to those who would not enter. (White, *Testimonies for the Church*, vol. 9, p. 97)

White was concerned for those who, like the unwise virgins, would find the door of mercy shut during the last hours of earth's history while it would remain open for others. One indication that probation hasn't closed for everyone during this period is that in the sixth plague, Christ Himself warns, "Behold, I come as a thief. Blessed is he that watcheth, and keepeth his garments, lest he walk naked, and they see his shame" (Rev. 16:15). If it is possible for believers to lose their wedding garments and be found naked, probation hasn't closed for them yet.

This is also confirmed two verses later, when the voice of God from the throne of heaven says, "It is done" (verse 17). That divine pronouncement is the final close for everyone, but notice, it occurs at the end of the Battle of Armageddon within the seventh plague.

ii   Adventists, from their beginning, have placed all seven trumpets of Revelation, except the last one, in the past, interpreting them as judgments on the Roman Empire (the first four) and then apostate

Christendom (the fifth and sixth.) This is a valid application, confirmed by the fall of the Ottoman Empire that was referenced in the first chapter, but Scripture and Ellen White do not confine themselves to a past application.

For example, the quote below is from an interesting letter by Ellen White written on December 22, 1890, from Washington, DC, to "Dear Children, Edson, Emma, and Willie." The first part of the letter gives her children the news of what she's been doing. The second half launches into a description of final events. Among many other interesting comments on the end times, she said the following:

> The power of the Holy Ghost must be upon us, and the Captain of the Lord's host will stand at the head of the angels of heaven to direct the battle. Solemn events before us are yet to transpire. Trumpet after trumpet is to be sounded, vial after vial poured out one after another upon the inhabitants of the earth. (White, *Manuscript Releases*, vol. 14, p. 287)

Notice the connection she made between the latter rain, the Battle of Armageddon, and the trumpets. If she had stopped at her statement that "trumpet after trumpet" will sound, we might be justified in questioning whether she was referring to the seven trumpets of Revelation 8–11. However, since she linked her comment on the trumpets to the vials (i.e., plagues), it is evident that she did mean what she seemed to be saying: that all seven trumpets and plagues apply to the end times and the trumpets will be repeated.

Below is another quote along the same lines, but in this one she linked the seals as well as the trumpets and plagues together and again placed all three in the future. The context of this statement is that she and some coworkers were caught in a severe thunderstorm in Australia, and the experience gave her forebodings of what end-time events will be like:

> My imagination anticipated what it must be in that period when the Lord's mighty voice shall give commission to His angels, "Go your ways, and pour out the vials of the wrath of God upon the earth" (Revelation 16:1).
>
> Thy right hand, O God, shall dash in pieces Thine enemies. Revelation 6 and 7 are full of meaning. Terrible are the judgments of God revealed.

The seven angels stood before God to receive their commission. To them were given seven trumpets. The Lord was going forth to punish the inhabitants of the earth for their iniquity, and the earth was to disclose her blood and no more cover her slain. Give the description in chapter 6. (White, *Manuscript Releases*, v. 15, pp. 219, 220)

Pay attention to the final sentence. What is in Revelation 6? The first six of the seven seals. Notice above how she linked the seals, trumpets, and plagues together, implying that all three are more or less concurrent.

iii Ellen White said this brief but impressive revelation of Christ's divinity was the reason even the bravest fled, and it makes sense: The temple guards, priests, and merchants, who were avaricious, would not ordinarily flee from a humble commoner holding a few fragments of rope. Christ's brief display of His divinity struck them with terror. White recounted this event:

With searching glance, Christ takes in the scene before Him as He stands upon the steps of the temple court. With prophetic eye He looks into futurity, and sees not only years, but centuries and ages. He sees how priests and rulers will turn the needy from their right, and forbid that the gospel shall be preached to the poor. He sees how the love of God will be concealed from sinners, and men will make merchandise of His grace. As He beholds the scene, indignation, authority, and power are expressed in His countenance. The attention of the people is attracted to Him. The eyes of those engaged in their unholy traffic are riveted upon His face. They cannot withdraw their gaze. They feel that this Man reads their inmost thoughts, and discovers their hidden motives. Some attempt to conceal their faces, as if their evil deeds were written upon their countenances, to be scanned by those searching eyes.

The confusion is hushed. The sound of traffic and bargaining has ceased. The silence becomes painful. A sense of awe overpowers the assembly. It is as if they were arraigned before the tribunal of God to answer for their deeds. Looking upon Christ, they behold divinity flash through the garb of humanity. The Majesty of heaven stands as the Judge will stand at the last day,—not now encircled with the glory that will then attend Him, but with the same power to read the soul. (White, *The Desire of Ages*, pp. 157, 158)

iv   There is one final stage of the antichrist that should be mentioned. At some point during the time of trouble, the final human antichrist will be replaced by Satan himself:

> As the crowning act in the great drama of deception, Satan himself will personate Christ. The church has long professed to look to the Saviour's advent as the consummation of her hopes. Now the great deceiver will make it appear that Christ has come. In different parts of the earth, Satan will manifest himself among men as a majestic being of dazzling brightness, resembling the description of the Son of God given by John in the Revelation. Revelation 1:13–15. The glory that surrounds him is unsurpassed by anything that mortal eyes have yet beheld. The shout of triumph rings out upon the air: "Christ has come! Christ has come!" The people prostrate themselves in adoration before him, while he lifts up his hands and pronounces a blessing upon them, as Christ blessed His disciples when He was upon the earth. His voice is soft and subdued, yet full of melody. In gentle, compassionate tones he presents some of the same gracious, heavenly truths which the Saviour uttered; he heals the diseases of the people, and then, in his assumed character of Christ, he claims to have changed the Sabbath to Sunday, and commands all to hallow the day which he has blessed. He declares that those who persist in keeping holy the seventh day are blaspheming his name by refusing to listen to his angels sent to them with light and truth. This is the strong, almost overmastering delusion. Like the Samaritans who were deceived by Simon Magus, the multitudes, from the least to the greatest, give heed to these sorceries, saying: This is "the great power of God." Acts 8:10.
>
> But the people of God will not be misled. The teachings of this false Christ are not in accordance with the Scriptures. His blessing is pronounced upon the worshipers of the beast and his image, the very class upon whom the Bible declares that God's unmingled wrath shall be poured out.
>
> And, furthermore, Satan is not permitted to counterfeit the manner of Christ's advent. The Saviour has warned His people against deception upon this point, and has clearly foretold the manner of His second coming. "There shall arise false Christs, and false prophets, and shall show great signs and wonders; insomuch that, if it were possible, they shall deceive the very elect.... Wherefore if they shall say unto you, Behold, He is in the desert; go not forth; behold,

He is in the secret chambers; believe it not. For as the lightning cometh out of the east, and shineth even unto the west; so shall also the coming of the Son of man be." Matt. 24:24–27, 31; 25:31; Rev 1:7; 1 Thess. 4:16, 17. This coming there no possibility of counterfeiting. It will be universally known—witnessed by the whole world.

Only those who have been diligent students of the Scriptures and who have received the love of the truth will be shielded from the powerful delusion that takes the world captive. By the Bible testimony these will detect the deceiver in his disguise. To all the testing time will come. By the sifting of temptation the genuine Christian will be revealed. Are the people of God now so firmly established upon His word that they would not yield to the evidence of their senses? Would they, in such a crisis, cling to the Bible and the Bible only? Satan will, if possible, prevent them from obtaining a preparation to stand in that day. He will so arrange affairs as to hedge up their way, entangle them with earthly treasures, cause them to carry a heavy, wearisome burden, that their hearts may be overcharged with the cares of this life and the day of trial may come upon them as a thief. (White, *The Great Controversy*, pp. 624, 625)

v Some Adventists will have an issue with making a connection between the King of the North, spiritual Babylon, and the antichrist because of Ellen White's many ringing endorsements of Uriah Smith's book *Daniel and the Revelation*. In it, Smith said at the end, the King of the North is Turkey. To those with that objection, I'd suggest her endorsements of Smith's book (which is an excellent book and a resource I often reference) need to be qualified by her other statements, general and specific.

Regarding her general statements, White made it clear that we have more to learn and unlearn with respect to prophecy.

> It is necessary that our unity today be of a character that will bear the test of trial.... We have many lessons to learn, and many, many to unlearn. God and heaven alone are infallible. Those who think that they will never have to give up a cherished view, never have occasion to change an opinion, will be disappointed. As long as we hold to our own ideas and opinions with determined persistency, we cannot have the unity for which Christ prayed. (White, *Testimonies to Ministers and Gospel Workers*, p. 30)

The above statement was written in 1888, twenty-one years after Smith's book was first published. Regarding White's specific statements, notice the following:

> We have no time to lose. Troublous times are before us. The world is stirred with the spirit of war. Soon the scenes of trouble spoken of in the prophecies will take place. The prophecy in the eleventh of Daniel has nearly reached its complete fulfillment. Much of the history that has taken place in fulfillment of this prophecy will be repeated [Notice that this repetition of history is not covered by Smith in his book]. In the thirtieth verse a power is spoken of that "shall be grieved, and return, and have indignation against the holy covenant: so shall he do; he shall even return, and have intelligence with them that forsake the holy covenant." ....
>
> Scenes similar to those described in these words (Dan. 11:30–36) will take place. We see evidence that Satan is fast obtaining the control of human minds who have not the fear of God before them. Let all read and understand the prophecies of this book, for *we are now entering upon the time of trouble spoken of* .... (White, *Manuscript Releases*, vol. 13, p. 394, emphasis added)

> We are standing on the threshold of great and solemn events. Many of the prophecies are about to be fulfilled in quick succession. Every element of power is about to be set to work. *Past history will be repeated; old controversies will arouse to new life, and peril will beset God's people on every side.* Intensity is taking hold of the human family. It is permeating everything upon the earth....
>
> Study Revelation in connection with Daniel, for history will be repeated.... We, with all our religious advantages, ought to know far more today than we do know [This was written in 1888, several years after *Daniel and the Revelation* was published]....
>
> A message that will arouse the churches is to be proclaimed. Every effort is to be made to give the light, not only to our people, but to the world. *I have been instructed that the prophecies of Daniel and the Revelation should be printed in small books, with the necessary explanations, and should be sent all over the world. Our own people need to have the light placed before them in clearer lines* [This was written in 1898]. (White, *Testimonies to Ministers and Gospel Workers*, pp. 116, 117, emphasis added)

vi   Daniel 11:45 describes the overthrow of the King of the North, who I suggest is the eighth head and ten horns at this point. In the next scene, at the beginning of chapter 12, Michael stands up, but the two scenes are concurrent. Daniel 7:7 is the parallel passage to 11:40–45 and Daniel 12:1–4: The time when Michael stands up is the same as when Christ is glorified and crowned, the judgment is set in heaven, and the little horn is judged.

Both occur during the height of persecution when the King of the North enters and assaults the "glorious land." This assault is when the little horn is speaking great words and wearing out the saints of the Most High. The King of the North comes to his end because he is fighting God Himself when Michael stands up.

Further evidence that the power described in Daniel 11:36–45 cannot be Revolutionary France, as some claim, is that: 1) Ellen White never made that application. Instead, she applied Revelation 11 to France during the Reign of Terror; and 2) verse 36 says this is the power that "shall prosper till the indignation be accomplished." And from Revelation 13 and 17, we know it is the eighth head of the beast, together with the ten horns, that executes the final assault on the people of God. The power at the end of Daniel 11 is therefore the same abomination of desolation that calls down the seven last plagues.

vii Armageddon, according to Ellen White in these and other statements, is the battle between the elements of good and evil under the outpouring of the latter rain. White's statements challenge us in more ways than one. For one, we have to ask ourselves just how prepared we are to meet the conflict when it comes.

Another challenge we have from her statements is the need to review our position on when the close of probation occurs: before, during or at the close of the battle. In some statements, she placed the close of probation at the end of the battle, but in others, she placed the close of probation at the commencement of the seven last plagues—an apparent contradiction. If Armageddon occurs during the sixth plague, probation must be closed by the commencement of the battle, not at the end of it, as she said above.

However, there has to be an underlying harmony. For one, Armageddon, although it reaches its climax under the seventh plague, apparently begins well before the plagues fall in full force. This is consistent with Christ's parable of the ten virgins, where probation closes earlier for the unwise virgins than for those wise virgins who trim their lamps and join the midnight cry.

If Armageddon is the final spiritual war under the ministry of the Holy Spirit, then when the loud cry of the third angel begins to sound, there is an initial close of probation for those who have already heard the message but have not been sanctified by it. Inspiration confirms this:

> The time of God's destructive judgments is the time of mercy for those who have had no opportunity to learn what is truth. Tenderly will the Lord look upon them. His heart of mercy is touched; *His hand is still stretched out to save, while the door is closed to those who would not enter.* (White, *Testimonies for the Church*, vol. 9, p. 97, emphasis added)

> Scenes similar to those described in these words will take place. We see evidence that Satan is fast obtaining the control of human minds who have not the fear of God before them. Let all read and understand the prophecies of this book, for *we are now entering upon the time of trouble spoken of* ... (White, *Manuscript Releases*, vol. 13, p. 394, emphasis added)

The parable of the ten virgins applies to us as Adventists. Probation closes for the five foolish virgins before it does for those who have not heard the loud cry message. The question for each of us is, Are we cooperating with the Holy Spirit? Do we have an extra supply of oil for our lamps?

TEACH Services, Inc.
P U B L I S H I N G

We invite you to view the complete
selection of titles we publish at:
www.TEACHServices.com

We encourage you to write us
with your thoughts about this,
or any other book we publish at:
info@TEACHServices.com

TEACH Services' titles may be purchased in
bulk quantities for educational, fund-raising,
business, or promotional use.
bulksales@TEACHServices.com

Finally, if you are interested in seeing
your own book in print, please contact us at:
publishing@TEACHServices.com
We are happy to review your manuscript at no charge.